General Editor:	David Jollands
Design Director:	Elwyn Blacker
Consultant Authors:	Paul Doherty
	Roy Edwards
	Alan Hibbert
	Jim Hudson
	John Little
	John Mason
	Cleland McVeigh
	Peter Metcalfe
	Beverley Moody
	Patrick Moore
	Michael Pollard
	Keith Porter
	Tim Pridgeon
	Derek Slack
	Ian Soden
	Tony Soper
	Alan Thomas
Research Editor:	Simon Jollands
Design and Production:	BLA Publishing Limited
	Michael Blacker
	Simon Blacker
	Margaret Hickey
	Alison Lawrenson
	Graeme Little
	David Oakley
	Lorrie Spooner
Artists:	Paul Doherty
	John Flynn/Linden Artists
	Hayward & Martin
	Richard Lewis
	Steve Lings/Linden Artists
	Jane Pickering/Linden Artists
	Chris Rotheroe/Linden Artists
	Eric Thomas
	Brian Watson/Linden Artists
	Phil Weare/Linden Artists
	Rosie Vane-Wright

SCIENCE UNIVERSE SERIES

EARTH, SEA AND SKY

ARCO PUBLISHING, INC.
NEW YORK

Acknowledgements

The publishers wish to thank the following organizations for their invaluable assistance in the preparation of this book.

Airships Industries (UK) Ltd
Austin Rover Group Ltd
British Caledonian
British Hovercraft Corporation Ltd
British Petroleum
British Robot Association
British Telecom
Canon (UK)
Central Electricity Generating Board
Cincinnati Milacron Ltd
Commodore (UK) Ltd
Disabled Living Foundation
Dundee University
Eaton (UK) Ltd
Ferranti plc
Ford Motor Company
Furuno Ltd
General Electrical Company plc

Japan Ship Centre
Kodak Museum
Longines
NASA
National Film Board of Canada
Omega Electronic
Philips International bv
The Plessey Company plc
Rediffusion Simulation Ltd
Rolls-Royce Ltd
Royal Greenwich Observatory
Royal Smeets Offset
Shell
Sony (UK)
Southern Positives and Negatives (SPAN)
Standard Telephones and Cables
United Nations Organization
US Information Service

Photographic credits

t = top   b = bottom   l = left   r = right   c = centre

Cover photographs: *tl, tc, bl, bc* ZEFA; *tr* Colorsport; *br* NASA.

Title page: ZEFA

4, 5*t*, 5*b* ZEFA; 6 NASA; 13*br*, 14*t* Institute of Geological Sciences; 15*tr* Paul Brierley; 16*t*, 16*c*, 17*b*, 20*l*, 20*r* ZEFA; 22*l* Institute of Geological Sciences; 22*r* ZEFA; 23*l* Institute of Geological Sciences; 23*tr* ZEFA; 24*l* Institute of Geological Sciences; 24*t*, 24*c*, 25*tl* ZEFA; 25*bl*, 25*r*, 26*l* 26*r*, 27*bl*, 27*br* Institute of Geological Sciences; 27*cr* ZEFA; 28*t*, 28*c*, 29*tr* Institute of Geological Sciences; 33*br*, 34*bl*, 34*tr*, 35*t*, 35*r*, 36*t*, 37*tl*, 37*cr*, 37*bl*, 38*l*, 38*r*, 39*l*, 39*r*, 40*b* ZEFA; 40*r* Institute of Geological Sciences; 41*bl*, 41*tr* ZEFA; 42*l*, 42*r*, 43*t*, 43*c*, 43*b* John Mason/NASA; 44*l*, 46*t*, 47*t*, 48*t*, 48*c*, 48*b*, 49*tr* ZEFA; 50*l* John Mason; 50*r*, 51*br*, 53*br* ZEFA; 54*bl*, 54*bc* University of Dundee; 55*t*, 55*b*, 56*l*, 57*l* ZEFA; 57*r* Mansell Collection; 59*t*, 59*b* ZEFA; 60 British Petroleum; 61*t* ZEFA; 61*b* NASA.

Published by Arco Publishing, Inc.
215 Park Avenue South, New York, N.Y. 10003

© BLA Publishing Limited 1984

First published 1984

Library of Congress Cataloging in Publication Data
Main entry under title:

Earth, sea, and sky

   (Science universe series; v. 7)

   Includes index.
   Summary: Discusses the earth's origin, structure, crust, continental drift, mountains, earthquakes, volcanoes, the water cycle, atmosphere, and climate.

   1. Geophysics – Juvenile literature. [1. Geophysics.
   2. Earth]

I. Arco Publishing.   II. Series.

QC806.4.E27   1984   551   84-6312
ISBN 0-668-06181-2

This book was designed and produced by
BLA Publishing Limited, Swan Court,
East Grinstead, Sussex, England.
A member of the Ling Kee Group
LONDON · HONG KONG · TAIPEI · NEW YORK · SINGAPORE

Phototypeset in Great Britain by
Southern Positives and Negatives (SPAN).
Color origination by Chris Willcock Reproductions,
Premier Graphics and Planway Ltd.
Printed and bound in The Netherlands by
Royal Smeets Offset BV, Weert.

Conversion table for units

Length

1 nanometer (nm)	= 0.000001 millimeter	= 0.000000001 meter (one-billionth of a meter)
1 millimeter (mm)	= 0.1 centimeter	= 0.03937 inch
1 centimeter (cm)	= 10 millimeters	= 0.3937 inch
1 meter (m)	= 100 centimeters	= 39.37 inches
1 kilometer (km)	= 1000 meters	= 3280.8 feet = 0.621 mile

Area

1 square kilometer = 0.3861 square mile

Capacity

1 liter = 1.0567 quarts

Volume

1 cubic centimeter (cc) = 0.06102 cubic inch

Weight

1 kilogram (kg)	= 2.2 pounds	
1 metric ton	= 1000 kilograms	= 1.1 US tons

Contents

NOTE TO THE READER: while you are reading this book you will notice that certain words appear in **bold type**. This is to indicate a word listed in the Glossary on page 62. This glossary gives brief explanations of words which may be new to you.

Introduction

SEEN FROM SPACE, our world appears as a sphere surrounded by emptiness. Earth is the 'green' planet, clothed in plant life and half hidden in swirling clouds. Earth contains all the materials needed to provide food, and an **environment** for all living **organisms**. Yet Earth has not always been such a friendly place.

Far back in time when Earth was forming and cooling down, it did not have the protective shield of gases which we call the **atmosphere**. As Earth cooled, water vapor **condensed** as rain to create shallow seas and rivers. Under the protective layers of water, simple living organisms could then develop. This was the start of the long road towards 'green Earth'.

The first simple plants used the less harmful rays of the Sun to produce their food. As a by-product of the process, a gas called **oxygen** was produced which was to become an important part of our atmosphere. This gas also played a part in shielding the Earth from the harmful parts of the Sun's rays. The Sun still remains the

The Antarctic ice-sheet covers an area about one and one-half times that of the USA. In places, the ice has a thickness of 4 km. Despite this massive volume of frozen water in the Antarctic alone, both polar ice-caps together account for only about 2 per cent of our planet's water.

source of all the Earth's **energy**. Sunlight is used by green plants to make the basic foods upon which all life depends. The heat it sends out gives the Earth its weather systems and produces changes which we call seasons.

Earth is the only **planet** in our solar system which appears to maintain life. This is because it is near enough to the Sun to receive warmth from its rays, but not too close to prevent the existence of life. The same mixture of over one hundred **elements** which together make up the rocks, air and living cells, are also present on other planets in the solar system. The important difference between Earth and the other planets is that Earth is just the right distance away from the Sun for water to exist as a liquid. This simple substance has influenced developments on Earth. As rivers and seas, water has helped to wear down the mountains and build them up again from **sediments**. As clouds, water protects many parts of the world from the scorching heat of the Sun. Finally, and most important to us, water is the liquid in which life began and on which it still depends.

The timescale of the Earth's development is measured in millions of years. Such great lengths of time are difficult to imagine. Scientists believe that Earth was formed between 4 and 5 billion years ago. The earliest forms of life have been found in rocks approaching 4 billion years old, so life must have begun fairly soon after Earth had cooled. In the time scale of

Earth, human beings like ourselves did not appear until some 30,000 years ago. This is a very small part of the total time that Earth has existed, but in that short time the human species has already made a great impression upon our planet. We have dug deep into the Earth in our search for metals and minerals. Our advances in the world of science have enabled us to explore the Earth's surface from space. Despite our short time on Earth, we know much about the way our world works.

There are about 500 active volcanoes in the world today, and of these between twenty and thirty erupt each year. Present-day volcanic activity gives us some indication of how hostile the Earth must have been 4.5 billion years ago, before life began. The temperature of this molten lava is 1200°C.

Life abounds between extremes of heat and cold, and results from millions of years of development. We may feel that environments like this one have existed for ever, but in terms of geological time our Earth has been constantly changing. The continents drift, the climate varies, the mountain ranges grow, and the forces of erosion act relentlessly.

The Earth in space

ALTHOUGH THE EARTH seems very large to us, it is really a rather small planet. It is one of the nine known planets. These and their moons, together with smaller bodies, such as **asteroids** and **comets**, make up our **solar system**.

The central body of the solar system, the Sun, is an ordinary star. Though its diameter is well over one million kilometers, it is still looked upon by astronomers as a **dwarf star** of below average size. The Sun is just one of 100 billion stars that make up our **galaxy**.

Our galaxy is a flattened, disk-shaped system of stars. It is so vast that astronomers have to use a unit of measurement called a **light-year** to describe it. A light-year is the distance that light travels in a year. The speed of light is 300,000 km per second. Our galaxy is almost 100,000 light-years from one end to the other. Our galaxy is so large that even the vast number of stars in it are two or three light-years apart from each other.

Despite this, our galaxy is only an average star system, though it is one of the larger members of the group of galaxies of which it is a part. This group is made up of about twenty or thirty galaxies in a cluster about five million light-years across.

As we look further into space, beyond the galaxy in which Earth is placed, we see many such groups of galaxies. Some are small like our

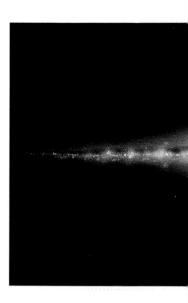

The Earth *(below)*, seen from a distance of 170,000 km in space, is a minute speck compared with the vastness of the universe.

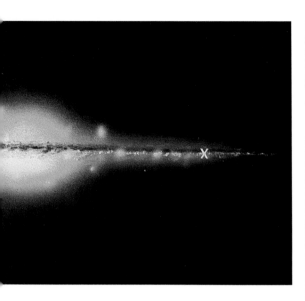

Our galaxy *(left)*, as it would be seen edge-on. The Sun and our own planetary system, marked X, lie away from the center. Our galaxy, which we call the Milky Way, is just one of millions of other galaxies.

The Sun and the nine planets compared, with their sizes to the same scale. To travel in a straight line at a steady 100 kph from our Earth to the Sun would take 170 years.

own, and some are vast, containing ten thousand galaxies or more. These clusters are thought to be members of even larger clusters, which between them make up the known universe. The universe contains more galaxies than there are stars in our galaxy. Those on the fringe of the universe, as scientists know it, are thought to be 8 billion light-years away from us here on Earth.

In all of this, the solar system of which Earth is a member becomes a very small pebble on a very large beach. Light could cross the solar system in 11.5 hours, could travel to us from the Sun in just over eight minutes, and from the Moon in 1.25 seconds. It could travel around the Earth in 0.125 of a second.

Planet Earth is our home in space. Like some huge spaceship, it contains a complete life support system, air to breathe, water to drink and food to eat. Better than any spaceship, our environment is one of endless variety in which to work and live and travel.

Where do all the materials which make up our planet come from? All these materials, including air and water, are known as **matter**. We use this word to describe anything that occupies space. All matter is made up of simple substances that cannot be broken down further, and these are known as elements. The Earth itself is made up of the same elements we find throughout the universe and inside the stars.

Of the known elements, ninety-two are found naturally on Earth and most of these have been detected in the Sun by scientists using an instrument called a **spectroscope**. This is an instrument used for breaking up light and for studying the colors of the spectrum. These vary from one element to another. One element, the gas helium, was first discovered in the Sun by this method, and only later found here on Earth.

7

The Earth's origin

THE SIMPLEST and lightest element, hydrogen, forms the basis of all elements, and therefore all matter. Heavier elements may be built up from hydrogen by **nuclear reactions**, at very high temperatures, inside the Sun and other stars. Scientists do not know whether these reactions took place at the very birth of the universe, the 'big bang', as it is sometimes called. They do, however, know that heavy elements are still being made inside stars, and it is likely that all the materials of the Earth were formed in this way.

Some stars actually explode as **supernovae**, spreading their materials through space to be collected into new star systems. This material is then used in the production of even heavier elements.

In the case of the solar system and our Earth, this all happened long ago. Scientists believe that the solar system was formed about 5 billion years ago, and the Earth itself about 4.5 billion years ago.

There are several theories or ideas how this could have happened. Scientists do not know for certain which processes were involved, because we cannot observe the events taking place in any other solar system. In fact, we only have the very slightest evidence that other planetary systems do exist. Certain stars have a

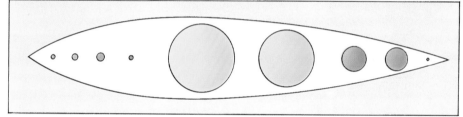

slight wobble in their movement through space. This may be evidence that planets, which we cannot observe, are in orbit around them. Barnard's star is a good example of such a pos-

The Jeans theory explaining the origin of our solar system *(above)* suggests that the planets were torn from the Sun by the passing of another star. This formed a cigar-shaped trail of planets with Jupiter in the center.

A more recent theory of how the solar system was formed proposes that the planets condensed from a disk of gas and dust thrown out from a massive, rapidly rotating Sun.

sibility. Also, quite recently, the Infrared Astronomy Satellite, IRAS, seems to have detected signs of solar systems forming around the stars Vega and Fomalhaut.

Until a few years ago the popular idea was one called the tidal theory. In 1916 the British astronomer James Jeans suggested that a star had come close to our Sun in the very distant past. This resulted in material from the Sun being drawn out into space, with the larger pieces forming the planets, including our own planet, Earth.

Although Jeans' theory accounts for the order of planet sizes, it is no longer taken seriously. More recent theories for the formation of the solar system are variations on one theme. These theories suggest that the planets formed as the Sun itself formed.

It is now thought that the Sun was formed from a large cloud of gas in space. This large cloud shrank under its own **gravity** to form a smaller, more tightly packed cloud. In time, due to pressure building up in the cloud, the newly-forming star began to heat up so much that nuclear processes started and the star began to shine.

The surrounding matter then formed itself into a disk, and the planets could have taken

shape within this disk in two ways. The first way is known by scientists as **accretion**. In this process, millimeter-sized grains of dust in the disk stuck together to form larger, centimeter-sized pieces. These then settled into the shape of a flattened disk around the Sun, becoming the future **plane** of the planets. These larger pieces then collided to form meter-sized – and in time, kilometer-sized – bodies. These collisions, though breaking up some of the bodies, formed others which went on to become the cores of the future planets. Because of gravity, the heaviest elements always sank to the center.

The second variation suggests that the **nebula** surrounding the Sun actually formed itself into smaller bodies. These would be large enough to form planets as they contracted under their own gravity.

Each of these theories suggests that the bodies from which the planets were formed would have taken up the surrounding gases and formed an atmosphere. The smaller planets, close to the Sun, soon lost their atmospheres because of the Sun's radiation. The more massive planets, being further away, were able to retain most of their original atmospheres. These were held to them, as in the case of the planet Earth, by their own gravity.

A variation of the disk theory of solar system evolution, suggests that the Sun and planets all formed at the same time, out of one condensing cloud of gas and dust.

The Earth's structure

THE EARTH is roughly spherical in shape but slightly flattened at the Poles. It has a radius at the equator of 6358 km, and a polar radius of 6357 km. It is made up of several shells, one inside the other. If you could cut the Earth in two, it would look rather like half of an onion with the layers appearing as a series of rings. Each shell has its own properties, depending on the rocks it contains and the conditions which exist at the depth of the shell. It is possible to divide the shells into three main regions. The outermost region, called the **crust**, is quite thin. You can imagine it as being like the skin on an apple. Beneath the crust is a layer called the **mantle**. The innermost part of all is the Earth's **core**.

Scientists have studied the rocks which make up the crust, both on the surface and at the bottom of deep mines. However, they can only find out about the Earth's interior by studying the paths of the **vibrations** caused by **earthquakes**.

Seismic waves spread outwards from an earthquake rather like ripples do if you throw a stone into a pond. However, the effect is more complicated. For one thing, the density of rock varies, unlike the density of water. Also, the pressures inside the Earth are so great that the waves tend to deflect back towards the surface. There are two types of seismic waves that penetrate the Earth. Primary waves (1) move faster than secondary waves (2) and penetrate the core. Studying these factors tells scientists much about the Earth's structure.

An earthquake is the name given to a violent shaking of the ground. The vibrations, or **seismic waves**, spread out in all directions from the point where an earthquake occurs. Some types of rock are more closely packed together than others. They are said to have a higher density. Whenever seismic waves cross the join between two rock layers having different densities, they are bent. This is similar to the way light waves are bent when passing from air into glass. If seismic waves hit the division between the two rock layers at a low angle, they are reflected instead.

Special observatories have been set up all over the world to record seismic waves. Those from a distant earthquake will tend to emerge steeply from the Earth's crust, but waves from nearby earthquakes will emerge at shallow angles. By measuring these angles from several observatories, scientists have learned a great deal about seismic waves. They can measure the speed at which they travel, their times of arrival, and the distances they travel. Using this information scientists are able to work out the positions and densities of the different rock layers which make up the Earth below the crust.

There are two kinds of crust: continental and oceanic. The continental crust is less dense than the oceanic, and is, on average, about 30 km thick. Beneath high mountain ranges its thickness may be more than 60 km. Very large areas of the continental crust are more than 1.5 billion years old. No part of the oceanic crust is older than 200 million years. The upper crust in continental areas is known as **sial**. This is because it contains mainly **si**licon and **al**uminum. The oceanic crust, and that underneath the sial in continental areas, is called **sima**. This is because it contains **si**licon and **ma**gnesium. The Earth's crust is less dense than the underlying mantle. This shows up in the way seismic waves are reflected.

The upper mantle consists of three layers. The thin, rigid top layer extends to a depth of between 60 km and 100 km. This is followed by a layer called the **asthenosphere**, extending down to about 200 km. Beneath this is a thick bottom layer, which extends to a depth of 700 km. The uppermost layer of the mantle and the crust are together called the **lithosphere**.

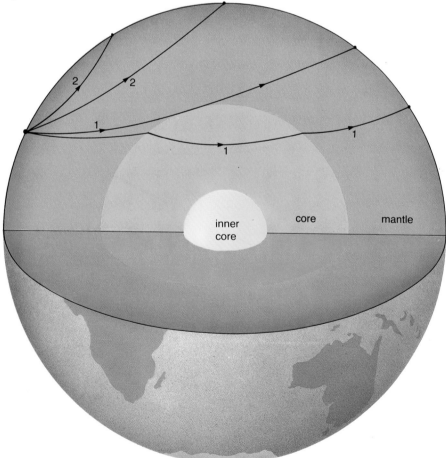

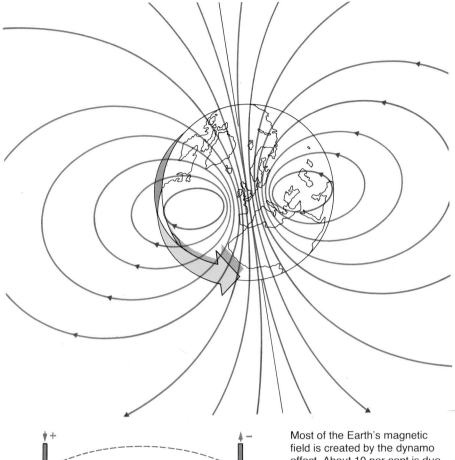

liquid, rock. The core itself is divided at a depth of 5150 km, and here the inner core begins. It is thought that the inner core is solid, consisting mainly of the metals iron and nickel. Although it is only 16 per cent of the Earth's volume, scientists believe that the inner core represents nearly one-third of its total mass.

As the Earth spins on its axis, the molten metal of the outer core allows the mantle and solid crust to rotate just a little bit faster than the inner core. Because of this difference, an electric current is set up within the core, rather like the current produced from the dynamo on the hub of a bicycle wheel as the wheel spins round. The electric current in the Earth's core produces a strong **magnetic field**.

The magnetic poles of the Earth do not coincide with the ends of the Earth's axis of rotation. Also, their position is continually changing. This is known as polar wandering.

Scientists studying very old rocks have found that rocks formed only a short time apart sometimes have completely opposite magnetic fields. This shows that the Earth's field must have turned completely around, with the north magnetic pole becoming south and the south magnetic pole becoming north. This is called a magnetic reversal. The same would happen if you reversed the direction of the electric current flowing in a large coil of wire. The Earth's magnetic field does not flip over suddenly. Its strength slowly falls to zero and then increases again in the opposite direction.

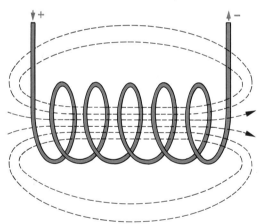

Most of the Earth's magnetic field is created by the dynamo effect. About 10 per cent is due to electrically charged particles coming from the Sun, and from magnetic rocks in the crust. The nature of the field is similar to that of a coil (left). It is more complicated because the Earth's field changes, and true north and magnetic north vary. The magnetic effect is greatest at the poles, and weakens towards the equator.

This is divided into a number of **plates**. Between the lithosphere and the asthenosphere the temperature and pressure are such that some of the rock is molten. The molten rock, or **magma**, forms a thin liquid layer on which the plates of the lithosphere can float, and drift sideways. This gives rise to **continental drift**.

The upper mantle is separated from the lower mantle by yet another division. Here rock density again increases, and the mantle is composed mainly of a rock which is heavy and dark in color. The lower mantle also contains other rocks, which are even heavier and are formed as a result of the tremendous crushing pressures of the rocks above them. The lower mantle extends to a depth of 2900 km.

The Earth's outer core is made of molten, or

Magnetic reversals occur very slowly. The magnetic strength first decreases until a point is reached when the field begins to reverse. The scale on the right shows variations in the Earth's magnetic field over 4 million years.

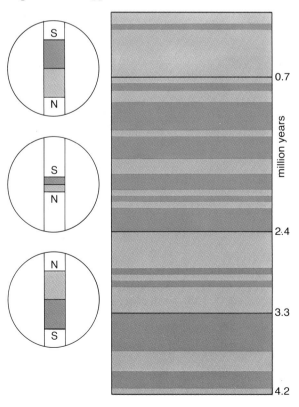

The Earth's crust

THE SOLID SURFACE of the Earth on which we live and work is just a thin crust. It lies above an inner layer called the mantle.

The crust, which floats on the mantle because it is lighter, is made of a number of plates. These plates may be hundreds, or even thousands, of kilometers across. Although all are lighter than the mantle on which they float, the density varies from plate to plate. They are pushed in various directions by the **convection currents** in the mantle.

Where the material in the crust is dense, the crust is thin, 6 km or so, and it floats low over

At other edges of the plates we find areas where the plates are moving together. Here, the lighter plate rides up over the heavier one, which is usually thinner and bends more easily. Where this occurs at the edge of a **continental shelf**, the continent rides over the heavier seabed.

The area where the crust is forced down is called a **subduction zone**. As the crust is pushed down into the mantle, it is melted by the increased temperature. Because the crust is lighter than the mantle, great masses of molten rock may rise through the mantle. They begin to

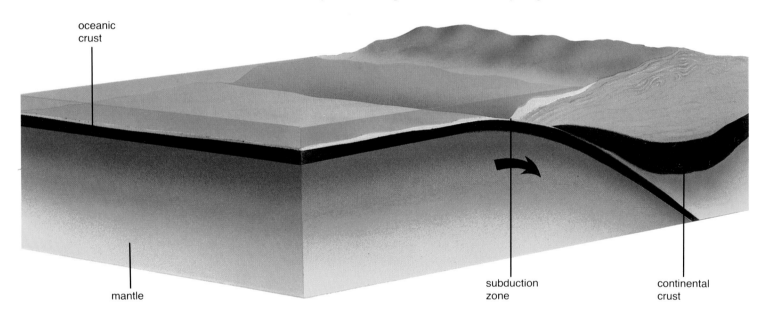

oceanic crust

mantle

subduction zone

continental crust

A subduction zone bordering a continent. The diagram shows one plate of oceanic crust being deflected beneath a plate of continental crust.

the mantle. Here, oceans have formed on top. Where the crust is lighter, it is thicker, up to 70 km thick in the mountainous areas. It is these thicker areas which form the continents on which we live.

In the thin areas under the oceans, the crust is weaker. It is here that new crust is being formed and old crust destroyed. The ocean **ridges** mark joints between the plates, where they are moving apart, and the molten material from underneath is welling up. The rocks around the ridges can be dated by their magnetic fields. These indicate where the magnetic poles were when the plates were formed. The Earth's magnetic field reverses every few hundred thousand years, changing the direction of the magnetic field in the rocks. The rocks become older further away from the ridges.

melt their way through the lighter rocks above the subduction zone. Some of this molten material may push its way to the surface and form volcanic regions like those on the western sea coast of North America.

The continental regions have a layered structure with the lighter layers on top. These are mainly granite and rocks that have been melted and re-formed. These are known as **metamorphic** rocks. The other types of rock are formed by **erosion** (wearing away). For example, sandstone is formed in this way. Some rocks, such as limestone, are formed from the dead remains of microscopic organisms. These other types of rock form only a small part of the crust. However, they appear to be common only because they are all at the surface, where we can see them.

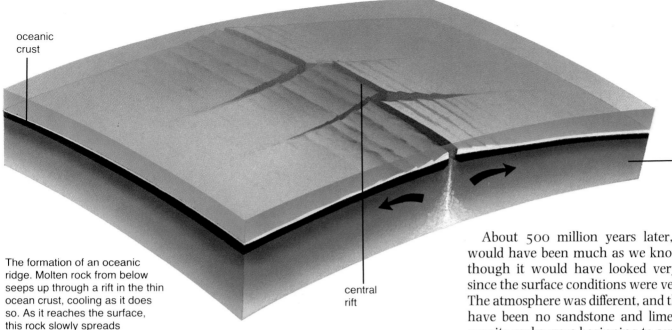

oceanic crust

mantle

central rift

The formation of an oceanic ridge. Molten rock from below seeps up through a rift in the thin ocean crust, cooling as it does so. As it reaches the surface, this rock slowly spreads outwards, at a rate of between 1 and 10 centimeters each year.

The Earth's surface over 4.5 billion years ago was semi-molten. A crust only began to form as the Earth cooled. Frequent eruptions took place as the molten material was forced up by pressures from below.

The Earth's crust was formed about 4.5 billion years ago as the young planet started to cool down from the energies of its formation. The early crust would have had very little variation in structure and shape. It would have been made up mainly of the **basalt** rocks of the mantle. It was probably composed of many small plates, and was continuously bombarded by **meteorites**, from space. The surface was still very hot and there would have been no surface water to break up the different kinds of rock.

About 500 million years later, the crust would have been much as we know it today, though it would have looked very different, since the surface conditions were very strange. The atmosphere was different, and there would have been no sandstone and limestone. The granite rocks were beginning to separate from the heavier basalt of the mantle, by melting and re-forming. This process slowly separates the lighter rocks which form the continental parts of the crust today. The crust would still be very thin and the activity of volcanoes much higher than at the present day.

In the 4 billion years since then, the crust has changed little, though volcanic eruptions and earthquakes still occur in certain areas. The crust now appears to be stable and settled, and is likely to remain so for the next few million years.

Seas and oceans

450 million years ago the seas were very different from today. They were shallower and frequent volcanic eruptions occurred.

AS THE PLANET EARTH was forming from a swirling cloud of hot gases and dust, the heaviest materials went to the core of the globe and the lightest remained on the outside. Among the lightest were the gas carbon dioxide, and water vapor, which formed part of the first atmosphere. Once the outer surface of the Earth cooled, some of the water vapor formed clouds, and the first rain fell on the land. The first seas which formed were almost certainly fresh water. Many millions of years passed before sufficient **salts** had been dissolved out of the rocks to turn these seas into the salty oceans we know today.

The early seas, which once covered most of the Earth's surface, were probably quite shallow, as the formation of continents had not yet begun. The fossil record of those ancient times tells us that life began in these seas and continued to thrive. The great mountain building activity took place about 400 million years ago. Extensive swamps were formed during the **Carboniferous** period of 300 million years ago. Evidence for this lies in the vast deposits of coal, oil and gas which we find in various parts of the world. These were made from the decaying plants which grew and died in such swamps.

The oceans as we know them today are quite recent in the history of the Earth. They were created as the continents formed, and were in many ways the reason for the movement of land masses, or **continental drift**. The rocks of the continents are very much older than those at the bottom of the present-day oceans. This **oceanic crust** is still being produced as undersea volcanoes force up molten rock from deep

Between continents, the sea bed slopes gradually until it meets the edge of the continental shelf at a depth of 200 m. It then dips sharply to as much as 5000 m where it flattens out into a submarine plain. From the plain, volcanic seamounts and ocean ridges rise, occasionally breaking the surface as volcanic islands. The ridges are broken by faults and deep trenches, some over 10,000 m deep.

| seamount | ocean ridge | volcanic island | trench | continental slope | continental shelf |

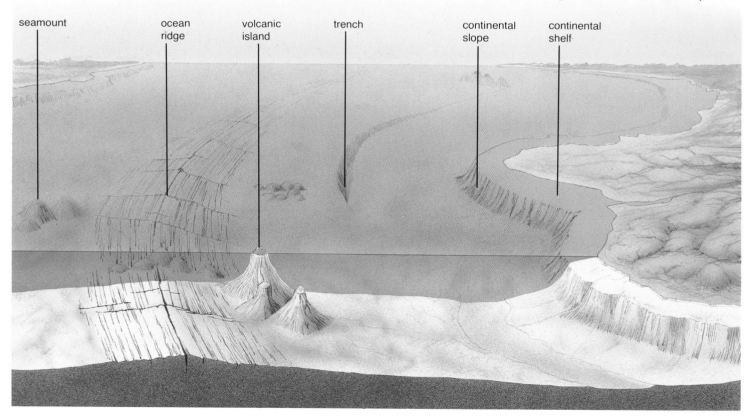

within the Earth. These volcanoes appear along lines, or ridges, on the ocean floor and spread out new rocks on either side. The ocean floor is growing outwards from these ridges at the rate of about 10 cm every year.

Today's oceans are very much deeper than the first seas. The pressures created by the movement of the oceanic crust create very deep gashes, or **trenches** on the ocean floor. The deepest trench in the world is the Marianas Trench near the Philippines in the Pacific Ocean. It is over 11 km deep. By comparison, the highest point on land is the summit of Mount Everest, which is 8.8 km above sea level. Not all of the ocean floor is new. Around the edges of the continents are extensions which were once the floors of ancient seas. These are known as the continental shelf and may extend 320 km from the shore. Above the continental shelf the ocean is very shallow, usually no more than 200 m deep. The edges of the shelf slope away very quickly to depths of 3000 m.

The ocean floor was almost unexplored until fairly recently. The first sailing ships charted the oceans by means of a lead weight on the end of a great length of line. This was lowered into the sea until it touched the sea bed and the depth was measured from the amount of line used up.

Knowledge of the ocean depths is built up by a variety of instruments and remote-controlled devices. Data and samples are collected by scientists aboard a research ship. Mapping of the sea bed is made possible by echolocation. The data gathered can be fed through a computer to produce a three-dimensional image *(right)*.

1 Dredger
2 Current meter
3 Unmanned submersible
4 Grab
5 Submerged buoy for measuring currents, temperature and salinity
6 Core sampler

In the 1900s, a device called an **echo sounder** was used to send a sound wave down to the sea floor. The reflection, or echo, of this sound was picked up by a sensitive microphone. The time between the sound being sent out and the echo received was used to measure the depth of sea.

Modern methods of charting the ocean floor involve the use of very powerful sounds which penetrate the softer sediments and even the rocks. This is called **seismic profiling**. The reflected sound waves enable us to build up a picture of the depth and structure of the ocean

floor. A similar technique is also used on land to search for deposits of oil and gas. These methods of exploration have helped to build up a very clear picture of ocean floors and show us that they have the same sort of volcanic peaks and deep canyons that we find on dry land.

We are still ignorant of what the deepest parts of the oceans are like. At such depths there is no light and the water is extremely cold. The main problem that restricts exploration is the tremendous pressure at the bottom of the deepest oceans. A pressure of one metric ton per square centimeter was recorded near the bottom of the Marianas Trench. Special diving vessels called **bathyspheres** are used to descend to great depths, but we still know less about the real ocean deeps than we do about space.

Waves and tides

Tides vary in height from place to place, some coasts having tides of over 12 m. In such places, a beached trawler at low tide would be a common sight. We would never see this in a land-locked sea such as the Mediterranean, where the tidal variation is only a few centimeters.

WAVES START in wind-blown water, forming what sailors call a 'sea'. The wind drives surface water before it, piling up smaller ripples into larger ripples. Most seas are only two or three meters high, though storms lasting for a long time over large expanses of water can produce very heavy seas indeed.

Although the crest of a wave can be seen moving forward, the water in a wave hardly moves at all. Each drop of water in a wave moves in a circle, as though on the rim of a revolving wheel. Deeper under the surface of the sea, these circles become smaller. Water deeper than the length of the wave is always still. Submarines can avoid the effect of heavy seas, even when they are quite near to the surface.

Waves do not move any water, but they do transfer energy. Because of this, there is little

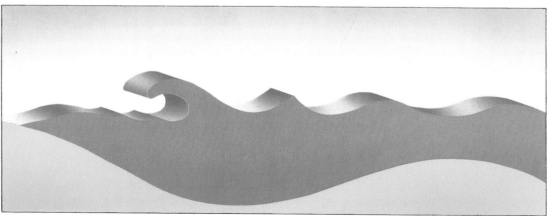

Waves are formed by wind blowing over the water. The water particles move in circular orbits. As a wave approaches the shoreline, it meets shallower water. The wave is unable to complete its circular movement and the crest breaks to form surf.

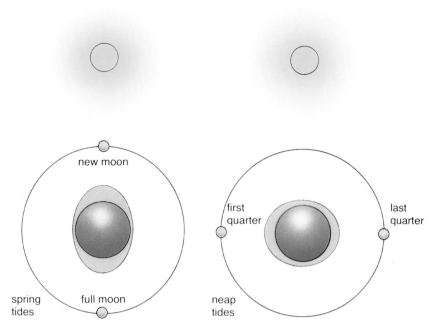

About twice a day the seas of the world surge from side to side in their ocean beds, piling up against one shore and then another. These tides are caused by the gravitational attraction of the Moon and to a lesser degree, of the Sun. This raises a bulge in the seas under the Moon. It also results in another bulge on the other side of the Earth, where the water is thrown out against gravity by **centripetal force**. There are usually two high tides and two low tides every twenty-four hours, but there are variations from one part of the world to another.

Not all tides have the same range. Near the time of the new and the full Moon, when the Sun, Moon and Earth are lined up, the tides are higher. These are called **spring tides**, and occur twice a month. The **neap tides**, which are very low, also occur twice a month when the Moon is in its first or last quarter. The height of the tide also varies from place to place. Small, land-locked seas, such as the Baltic and the Mediterranean, have very small tides, about 30 cm. On the other hand, some coastline shapes tend to funnel the waters and increase their range. At the inner end of the Bay of Fundy in Eastern Canada, the tide rises and falls 12 m.

friction and they travel long distances. As the waves travel further, they tend to flatten out, becoming widely spaced and faster-moving. A seaman calls this a swell. A swell can travel faster than the wind which raised it. In regions where waves from different directions cross, for example near the southern tip of Africa, they combine forces to build up very large swells indeed. Freak waves of 30 m or more have been reported in these areas.

As a wave approaches a shore, the drops of water circling at the bottom of the wave hit the ocean floor. This is called 'feeling bottom'. The resistance slows the wave down quite suddenly. The wave shortens, and the water at its crest often overtakes the front slope of the wave. This causes breakers and surf. The effect of the wave on the shore depends upon how far it has come. The long, fast, widely spaced waves that have crossed a vast expanse of ocean treat the shore more gently than the shorter, steeper and more frequent waves newly emerged from a storm. Waves from small expanses of sea are nearly always destructive.

The positions of the Moon and the Sun affect the tides. Twice a month, at new and full moon, the Sun, Moon and Earth are in line, and the high tides become higher. These are known as spring tides. When the Moon is in its first and last quarters, Sun, Moon and Earth form a right angle, causing only a small tidal variation. These are known as neap tides.

(right) All the water on the Earth's surface is pulled towards the Moon on the near side, and pushed away on the far side. This results in tidal bulges (high tides) at the nearest and farthest points.

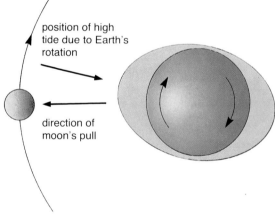

The shape of the coastline can change the pattern of the tides. The English port of Southampton, at the top of The Solent, has a very complex tide pattern. The tides fill and empty along both the narrow channels at opposite ends of the Isle of Wight. A violent example of tidal effects is in a strait called Moskenstraumen near the Lofoten Isles in Norway. Here the turning tide gives rise to a whirlpool called the Maelstrom. In ancient times this was a source of terror to the Vikings.

The tides contain huge amounts of energy, and there are a small number of power stations which use tidal energy to generate electricity. One of the best known is at St Malo in France. So far, this form of energy has not been widely used, since the power comes at inconvenient times, and is difficult to harness.

A large, long wave may break in the manner shown below when it passes over an area where the sea bed is shallow.

The drifting continents

THE LAND MASSES of the world can be divided into five main regions. These are Europe and Asia (sometimes called Eurasia), North and South America, Africa, Australasia and Antarctica. These land masses are called continents. Geographers in the seventeenth century realized that the different continents could be fitted together like pieces of a gigantic jigsaw puzzle. For example, the west coasts of Europe and Africa on one side of the Atlantic Ocean appear to fit with the eastern coastline of North and South America. In 1858, Antonio Snider-Pellegrini suggested that the continents were possibly once joined together, but then 'drifted' apart. However, at the time, there was little evidence to support this idea.

At the start of the twentieth century a German scientist and explorer, Alfred Wegener, decided to search for more definite proof that the continents had drifted apart. During his travels, he noticed that certain fossil bones from South Africa and South America were similar. These fossils were probably from a reptile called a *Mesosaurus*, found nowhere else on Earth. Wegener also found fossils of a leaf called *glossopteris*. These were found in rock deposits of the same age in South Africa, South America, India and Australia. Wegener thought that these examples provided evidence that **continental drift** had taken place.

The distribution of fossil leaves of *glossopteris* (brown) provided Alfred Wegener with evidence for his theory of continental drift. This plant fossil is only found in rocks 250 million years old, when continents, now separated, were thought to be joined. 50 million years ago, as this map shows, the continents looked very much like they do today.

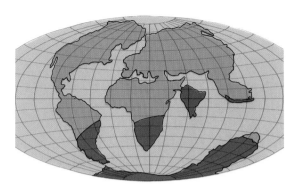

Wegener put forward the idea that all the continents long ago joined together in a single, vast super-continent. He called this land mass *Pangaea*, from the Greek meaning 'all land'. About 175 million years ago, *Pangaea* started to break apart into several smaller pieces, along the lines of today's continents. Since that time the pieces have slowly drifted apart. The Americas moved west, Asia north, Antarctica south, and Australasia east. Europe and Africa moved only slightly.

Looking at maps, Wegener imagined the Americas joined with Europe and Africa. When he did this, he noticed that mountain ranges would be linked in continuous chains. The Cape Mountains in South Africa appeared to continue south of Buenos Aires in Argentina. Mountains in eastern Canada linked up perfectly across the Atlantic Ocean with others in Scotland and Norway.

In the 1950s, scientists studied the magnetic properties of ancient rocks and found final proof of Wegener's theories. The Earth behaves like a huge magnet, and is surrounded by a magnetic field. When certain rocks are formed, they take up the properties of the Earth's magnetic field which surrounds them. Millions of years later scientists can look at these magnetized rocks and see where they were located within the Earth's magnetic field, when they were formed.

Some rocks in England, formed 200 million

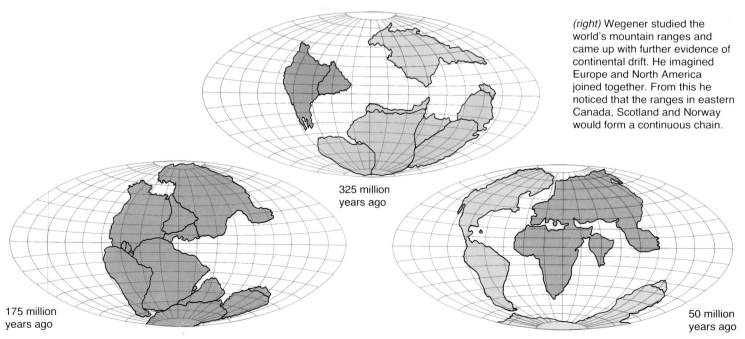

325 million
years ago

175 million
years ago

(right) Wegener studied the world's mountain ranges and came up with further evidence of continental drift. He imagined Europe and North America joined together. From this he noticed that the ranges in eastern Canada, Scotland and Norway would form a continuous chain.

50 million
years ago

The Earth's outer shell is made up of several large plates. These are slowly moving in the directions shown by the arrows. The boundaries of these plates mostly occur where there are spreading ridges on the ocean floor, or subduction zones along the coastal fringes of continents. These plate boundaries also coincide with belts of volcanic and earthquake activity.

—————— collision zone
⊥⊥⊥⊥⊥⊥ converging boundary
—⌐_⌐— diverging boundary
— — — — uncertain boundary

years ago, were magnetized as though they were then nearer the equator than they are today. In India, layers of rock, one on top of the other, had different magnetic properties. These properties changed with the age of the rocks. Those formed 150 million years ago were magnetized as though they had been close to the South Pole at that time. Younger layers of rock showed that India had apparently moved steadily north, crossing the equator about 25 million years ago. After much argument, scientists finally agreed that continental drift had indeed taken place, and is continuing even today.

Recently, scientists have formed new theories of the powerful forces which cause continental drift. The Earth's crust is broken up into several large, flexible sections, each about 100 km thick. These are called **tectonic plates**. The ocean basins and the continental land masses ride on top of these plates. These large plates are in continual movement. The tremendous heat energy given out from the Earth's core, heats material deep in the mantle and causes it to rise. This forces the plates apart. Elsewhere, cooler mantle material is dragged downwards towards the core. This causes the crustal plates to be pulled together and even drawn downwards into the mantle. There they are consumed by the intense heat and pressure. The rising and falling of hot and cool mantle material is called a **convection cycle**.

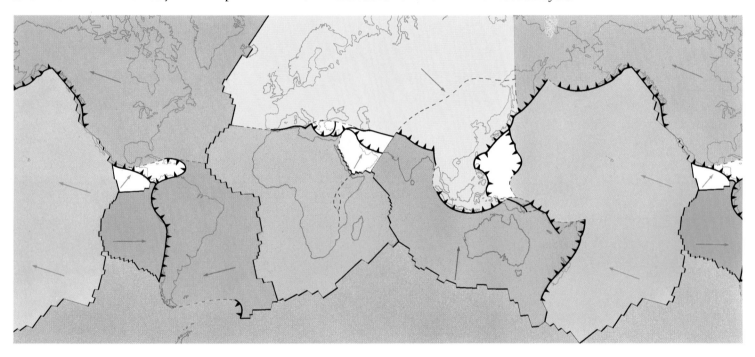

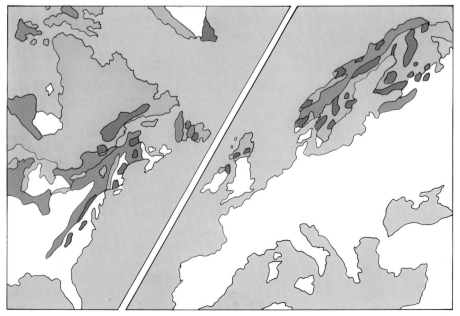

The Earth's crust remains in a more or less steady state. As plate material is destroyed, so new material is formed. Hot mantle material rises. This forces the plates apart along the lines of the **mid-ocean ridges**. Here the molten rock, or magma, flows to the surface from a central canyon running the length of the ridge. As it hardens, it fills the gap, forming new crust material. This causes the ocean floor to spread away from the ridge. This is known as **sea-floor spreading**. Along the mid-Atlantic ridge this process is pushing the plates, carrying the Americas gradually westward, away from those supporting Europe and Africa. It is like a gigantic conveyor belt slowly rolling the two land masses apart. In the eastern Pacific Ocean, 10 cm of new crust are added every year. Elsewhere, the rate of sea-floor spreading is between 1 and 8 cm per year.

Mountains are born

AMONG THE PEAKS of the world's highest mountains are layers of rock which contain the fossil remains of ancient sea organisms. How did rocks containing animals which lived on the sea bed end up thousands of meters above sea level? The answer is that these rocks, now at the tops of mountains, have been lifted up from the sea bed by tremendous forces. They are the result of collisions between neighboring continental plates. These plates are 'floating' on the rocks of the mantle beneath them. Great upheavals in the Earth's surface occur where the plates push against each other.

Millions of years before the Alps formed in Southern Europe, a great sea existed to the south of the European continental plate. The rivers of Europe washed down great thicknesses of different types of rock, such as clay and sandstone. The layers which formed are called **sedimentary rocks**. The sediments are always to be found at the edges of the continental plates. Some 20 million years ago, the plate supporting Italy slowly pushed into the underside of Eu-

The highest mountain in the world is Mount Everest (8848 m) in the Himalayas. It was formed 15 million years ago. Over 180 million years ago, India moved steadily north-east until it was forced into the underside of the Asian continental plate. This collision raised the great Himalayan mountain range. To us, these mountains may seem very old, but in geological time they are quite young.

The Jungfrau (left) is one of the highest peaks in the Alps at 4158 m.

rope. When two plates collide, the thrust of one on to the other forces the sedimentary rocks up between them. The rocks are crushed, and the crust containing the sedimentary rocks is pushed upwards to build high mountain ranges, such as the Alps. It is in these sedimentary rocks that the remains of ancient sea organisms are found.

The Rocky and Andes mountain ranges stretch down the west side of North and South America. The way in which these have been formed is rather different from that of the Alps and Himalayas. The plates supporting the American continents have drifted slowly westwards. In doing so, they have been driven against the eastern side of the huge Pacific plate. Two things have happened.

Firstly, the leading edges of the two American continents have been crumpled and folded along their entire length. This has built up the

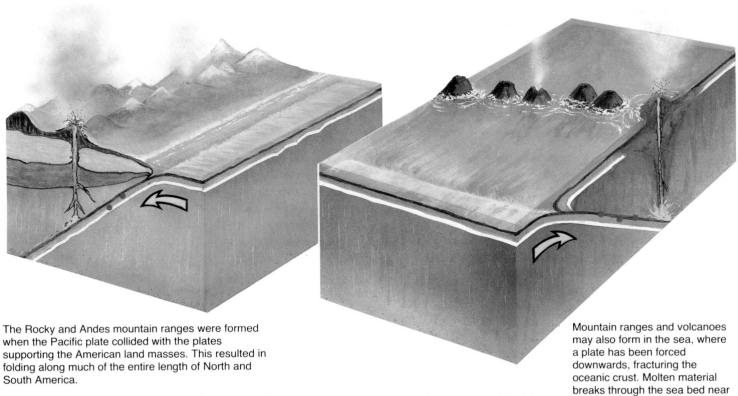

The Rocky and Andes mountain ranges were formed when the Pacific plate collided with the plates supporting the American land masses. This resulted in folding along much of the entire length of North and South America.

Mountain ranges and volcanoes may also form in the sea, where a plate has been forced downwards, fracturing the oceanic crust. Molten material breaks through the sea bed near the plate boundary. As a result, a chain of volcanic islands, called an island arc, is created.

Rocky and Andes mountains, which stretch from Alaska, in the north, to Cape Horn, in the south. Secondly, the oceanic crust of the Pacific plate has been forced underneath the plates supporting the Americas. It has been pushed deep into the rock of the mantle. There, it is steadily broken up and melted by the intense heat and pressure. The molten crust material, formed by this destruction of the Pacific plate, rises towards the Earth's surface. Here, it forms a line of **volcanoes** along the top of the high Andes mountain range. Where one plate is being pushed underneath another, intense earthquake activity is common.

It has been known for a long time that high mountain ranges, volcanoes and earthquakes occur in broad bands, stretching around the world. These bands mark the edges of the great plates in the Earth's crust. One such belt goes around the Pacific Ocean. It is sometimes called the 'ring of fire'. Another band stretches from South East Asia across to the Mediterranean Sea. Within it lie the Himalayas and the Alps. The third band lies along the mid-ocean ridge. This runs roughly north to south in the center of the Atlantic Ocean.

Great mountain ranges and lines of volcanoes do not form only on land. Beneath the Pacific Ocean, in the 'ring of fire', there are places where the Pacific plate is being pushed down into the mantle. At a depth of about 700 km, the oceanic crust is destroyed. Being less dense than the mantle, the molten crust material, or magma, rises towards the sea bed.

Here, it spurts out into the ocean and builds up lines of volcanic islands at the edge of the overriding plate. These are called **island arcs**. Japan, Hawaii and the Aleutian Islands are examples of where this has happened. Mauna Kea, in Hawaii, is actually the world's tallest mountain. Measured from the ocean bed to its peak, the total height is 10,023 m, of which 4205 m are above sea level. Along the line of the mid-Atlantic Ocean ridge, new crust is being formed. This new material is pushed up to form a line of mountains under the sea. This stretches from the north of Iceland nearly to Antarctica. In some places, the mountain tops rise to the ocean surface. There, they form islands, such as the Azores, Ascension and Tristan da Cunha.

Movements of the Earth's crust sometimes cause lines of weakness in the crust. These are called **faults**. Along the line of the fault, one block of crust will slide past the other. Where land on one side of the fault rises above the general ground level of the other side, **block mountains** are formed. An example is the Sierra Nevada, in the United States. Sometimes, land between two parallel faults will drop downwards. This forms a long, deep valley. The longest is the East African Rift Valley, which is 6400 km from end to end. The Red Sea lies inside this fault. Along the San Andreas fault, on the west coast of the United States, two continental plates are moving sideways past each other. Occasionally, the two sides of the fault get stuck together. If, later, they suddenly unstick again, an earthquake will occur.

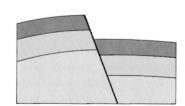

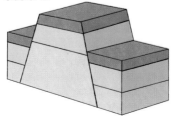

A simple fault (above) is caused when one block of crust slides below another along a line of weakness. A block mountain (below) is formed where an area is raised with faults on either side of it.

Chemicals in Earth, sea and sky

THE WORLD is really made up of three regions, Earth, sea and sky. Each of these regions contains different chemicals. The part of the Earth near the surface is called the crust. It is about 40 km deep and is made largely of rock. The two most common elements found in the crust are oxygen and silicon, the oxygen combining with other elements to form **compounds** known as **oxides**. Together, oxygen and silicon make up more than half of the crust, including the part we live on, and can see.

Many metals are found as oxides in the crust, and the commonest metal is aluminum. Because it is difficult to separate from oxygen, aluminum as a metal was hardly known before the twentieth century, although the compounds of aluminum are very common. Iron is the next most common metal, often giving color to compounds of other elements. Calcium, which is found in chalk, is next. The chalk was formed from the remains of microscopic animals which died millions of years ago.

Other metals in the Earth's crust are sodium, potassium and magnesium. Strangely, however, all the other elements make up only a tiny part of the total.

The material that lies beneath the crust, in

The temperature beneath the Earth's crust is so high that it melts the rock. Under great pressure, the molten rock is forced out of a crack in the crust, resulting in an erupting volcano. Showers of lava can reach as high as 300 m. During the eruption, the lava flows over the rim of the crater to form a lava flow.

Chalk, which contains calcium, a common metallic element found in the Earth's crust, was formed millions of years ago from the shells of marine animals. The piece of chalk shown here contains fossilized limpets.

the mantle, is quite different and we only see it when a volcano erupts. The temperature of the rock under the crust is much higher than it is on the surface, increasing by about 20°C for every kilometer of depth. Scientists believe that the temperature at the center of the Earth may be as much as 20,000°C.

This means that even fairly close to the surface some of the rocks will be so hot that they are liquid. The molten rock is called magma, and, under the great pressure inside the Earth, it can be forced out of any weakness or crack in the crust. This is what happens when a volcano erupts. The liquid rock, when it emerges, is called **lava**.

Even lava, from far below the surface, contains a large amount of oxygen and silicon, but, closer to the center of the Earth, pure elements such as iron and nickel are thought to exist. They would be in the liquid state because the temperature is so high.

The oceans, seas and rivers make up the second of the three regions. Together, these cover 71 per cent of the Earth's surface. Water consists almost entirely of the elements oxygen and hydrogen, of which it is a compound. However, water also contains a great variety of other elements and salts. Of these, salt itself, a compound of sodium and chloride, is the commonest chemical. The oceans and seas contain enough salt to cover all the land surfaces of the world to a depth of 150 m.

Potassium, magnesium and calcium compounds are also found dissolved in the water. Other elements are far less common, and we often extract some of the rarer ones from sea water. Some seaweeds are able to take iodine out of sea water, and the first method used for obtaining iodine was to collect the seaweed which contained it.

The oceans are full of surprises. Sometimes, clusters of **nodules** of manganese are found, each one as big as a fist. The nodules also contain copper and nickel, two elements we are

rapidly using up. How they are formed is not certain, but it does seem that they grow around small objects, in much the same way that pearls are formed.

We have hardly used any of the vast store of chemicals in the sea, but, as deposits of metals such as copper, nickel and manganese become scarce, this is something we shall have to do.

The last of the three regions is the atmosphere. The gases found here consist mainly of nitrogen and oxygen, not combined with any other element, but in their free state. Nitrogen makes up almost four-fifths of all the atmosphere, while oxygen makes up just over one-fifth. The other tiny portion is made up of some unusual gases that hardly form any compounds at all. They are called the inert gases. The term 'inert' means that they do not react chemically with other elements.

The most common of the inert gases is argon, and we use it in several different ways. When sodium metal is made from salt, it is so reactive that we have to fill the apparatus with argon to stop the sodium forming compounds with other gases. Light bulbs are filled with argon to stop the thin wire **filament** from burning away.

Carbon dioxide is present only in tiny amounts, but it is vital to plants and animals. Plants use it to form sugars, which they store to

Salt, a compound of sodium and chloride, is a common chemical found in water. Workers are shown above raking up the salt from shallow pans. The sea water has evaporated to leave rich deposits.

Manganese nodules *(left)*, formed by processes that are still not fully understood, are found on the sea bed. They consist of rock surrounded by layers of metal oxide.

give energy when needed. Animals eat the plants and use the sugars. They then breathe out carbon dioxide. In this way the amount of this gas in the air is kept at a steady level.

We have a great variety of chemicals available to us in Earth, sea and sky. The living world uses these chemicals in order to survive, and we use a great variety for our industries. Despite this constant use, the balance of chemicals in the three regions stays very much the same.

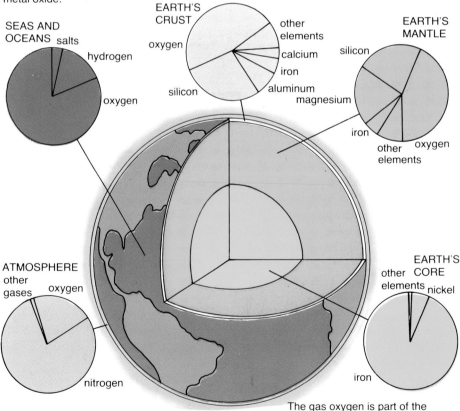

The elements, of which there are over 90, are the building bricks of all matter, including the atmosphere and the seas. Some of these elements occur more commonly than others.

The gas oxygen is part of the mixture known as air. It also combines with the gas hydrogen to form water. In the Earth's crust and mantle we find it again. Here it combines with other elements to form compounds known as oxides.

23

Rocks and minerals of the Earth

ANY SUBSTANCE that does not contain material which was once living, and is not man-made, can be called a mineral. Almost any rock is made up of several different substances. If you look closely at pieces of rock, you will probably see particles with differing colors and shapes. These different particles are known as minerals.

A piece of **granite**, for example, will usually contain three different minerals. Scratching the granite with a knife will sometimes reveal these. One is very hard, and looks rather like glass; it is called **quartz**. Black, shiny particles are probably **mica**, while pink or creamy-colored crystals are known as **feldspar**.

These minerals were formed as crystals when the hot, liquid rock from which they came cooled slowly. As they grew, the mixture of crystals produced different types of rock. Quartz is a compound of silicon, feldspar contains potassium, aluminum and silicon, while mica is made of compounds of iron and magnesium.

Granite is an example of an **igneous** rock, one that was once liquid, or molten. Granite consists of quite large crystals, because they were formed as the rock cooled slowly under the Earth's surface. Slow cooling always produces bigger crystals. Where the molten rock cooled faster on the surface of the Earth, very small crystals were formed, making a smooth, black rock called basalt.

Following a volcanic eruption, material exploded into the atmosphere settles back around the crater, or vents, of a volcano in layers known as tephra. The debris varies in size from fine dust to large boulders.

Basalts *(above)* are often divided into long uniform columns with four, five, six or more sides. These were formed as cooling basalt lava contracted. The Giant's Causeway in Ireland and the Devil's Postpile in California are well-known examples of this phenomenon.

Granite consists of grains (hence the name) of crystalline minerals. Amongst the white minerals are quartz (transparent), and feldspar (opaque). The black crystals include micas and amphibole.

Sandstone is a quite different kind of rock, made up of small particles which are round and smooth, like pebbles on a beach. These particles are embedded in a clay, and are more widely spaced out than the crystals in granite. Sandstone is also different from granite in the way in which it is formed. If you shake up some clay and sand in water, and then let them settle, the largest particles will form a layer at the bottom of the container, with smaller particles – the clay – slowly forming another layer on top of them. Now imagine this process repeated hundreds of times. The layers of rock formed in this way are called sandstone and **shale**. This type of rock, formed in rivers and lakes and in the sea, is called sedimentary rock.

Both types of rock can be changed to other minerals by a process called **weathering**. When oxygen and carbon dioxide are dissolved in rain water, they attack the chemicals in granite,

turning feldspar and mica into clay and **limonite**. Limonite is made from the dark-colored minerals which contain iron, and this stains the clay a yellow or brown color. Sedimentary rocks are broken up by weathering. When this happens the clay deposits are left behind as the sand is washed or blown away.

Scientists who study rocks are called geologists. Simple tests are used to help identify all the different forms of rocks and minerals. The shape of a crystal is only important when something very definite can be seen; crystals can be in the form of a cube or needle, or sometimes are scaly. Color is important, and it is best seen in a streak test, when the mineral is rubbed over a white background such as the back of a bathroom tile. **Luster**, the way a surface reflects light, is described as glassy, shiny, metallic or dull. The hardness of a mineral tells us something about the way the crystal is made up, and there is a scale of hardness of minerals. Some of the hardest minerals are called gems; diamond and sapphire are two examples.

One other test depends on how crystals split when they are struck. A geologist calls this **cleavage**. If mica is struck with a geologist's

Changes in climate can have a marked effect on the forces of erosion, as seen in the spectacular sandstone desert of Utah, USA. The main force that moulded this landscape was river erosion. The present-day scenery has been shaped by the additional activity of desert erosion.

Calcite crystals showing perfect cleavage are quite common. Calcite (calcium carbonate) occurs as limestone and marble.

hammer, it shows perfect cleavage with all the splits going in one direction only. In the case of calcite, cleavage can occur in three different directions, resulting in crystals which are cube-shaped.

What do we use minerals for? One use we make of them is based on the fact that many contain metals, in the form of compounds. If a mineral is used to provide us with a metal it is called an **ore**. The history of metals is fascinating – as people discovered more metals and how to use them, so civilization became more advanced. The earliest metals to be used were probably gold, silver, copper and lead. Gold and silver can be found as pieces of the metal, while

copper and lead are quite easily extracted from their ores by heating with charcoal. Iron and tin can also be prepared from their ores in this way, but we needed to wait for the discovery of electricity before metals such as calcium, magnesium and aluminum could be extracted.

Minerals are also used for coloring. The Chinese found a way of using clay and ground-up rock to make porcelain, and this was also discovered in Germany and England in the eighteenth century. Much of this porcelain was colored by using minerals which had been carefully separated from the rest of the rock in which they were found.

There are so many uses of rocks and minerals that it would be impossible to list them. They are the source of nearly all our metals, and of many non-metals. They provide us with many of the chemicals we use, apart from those which are based on carbon.

Limonite is a mineral composed of a mixture of iron oxides and hydroxides. It is formed by the weathering of minerals that contain iron.

Gemstones

PEOPLE have always decorated themselves and their possessions. Anything which sparkles and is colorful to look at has been used to attract. Apart from the bright metals, such as silver, copper and gold, there are several minerals which have been used for this purpose.

When minerals crystallize they take on particular shapes, and these shapes have sharp, clear edges and corners. This makes them glitter as they are moved, because light is reflected off the surfaces at different angles. Some minerals are transparent, and light is bent as it passes from one surface to another. This is called **refraction**, and it makes the crystal shapes attractive to look at.

There are many attractive mineral stones, and if they can be cut and polished they are often used as jewelry. Sapphires, emeralds, rubies, topazes and amethysts are just some of the jewels that have been known for thousands of years.

There is a difference between gems and semiprecious stones, and it is found in their hardness. Gems are very hard, and because of this they have been able to resist the normal weathering process that all rocks go through. Rocks become worn away over long periods of time. However, the hard crystals of gemstones resist this. Gradually they become washed into

Emeralds *(above)* are found in South America, South Africa and the USSR. They have been used for jewelry since ancient times.

Sapphires *(below)* are a form of the aluminum oxide mineral known as corundum. The blue coloring of sapphires is caused by small amounts of iron and titanium.

rivers, where they collect in areas called **placers**.

This may sound as though it is easy to find gemstones, but they are found only in very small quantities in certain parts of the world. Rubies come from Burma, Sri Lanka and Thailand, while sapphires are found in these countries and also in Kashmir, India. Emeralds come from South America, South Africa and the USSR. Once a deposit of these valuable gemstones is found, mining is quite easy. The problem is finding the deposit in the first place.

What are gemstones made of? They are crystals of common materials, and the crystals get their color from small amounts of **impurities** mixed in with the original chemical. Several of the best-known gemstones are made of aluminum oxide, which is normally a white powder with a very high melting point. If the aluminum oxide has cooled slowly so that it forms large, well-shaped crystals, sapphires and rubies are formed. Sapphires contain small amounts of iron and titanium, which give them their rich blue color, while rubies are colored red by chromium. The colorless crystals of aluminum oxide are not highly valued because they are much more common. Crystals like this are used in **emery** paper, which you can buy for rubbing down metal surfaces and for removing rust. Emery is the colorless or sometimes dark form of a mineral called **corundum**, and colored corundum is ruby or sapphire.

Diamonds are quite different. They are made of carbon which has crystallized in an almost perfect form, so strong that diamond tops the scale of hardness. Diamonds were formed millions of years ago when carbon, perhaps from trees trapped in volcanic eruptions, cooled very slowly and under enormous pressure from the rock surrounding it.

Other well-known stones, softer than gemstones but still quite hard, are forms of quartz, silicon dioxide. In this group of semi-precious stones are found amethyst, tiger's eye, agate and moonstone. Even iron and sulfur can form beautiful crystals. One crystal form of iron sulfide is called **pyrites**, and is a common ore of iron. It is sometimes called 'fool's gold' because of its color and luster. The other crystalline form of the same chemical is known as **marcasite**.

Gemstones have always been used for decoration, and sometimes instead of money. In recent times, low quality stones have been used for drilling, cutting and grinding, because of their hardness. Diamonds and rubies can be made in the laboratory; though the stones are small and of poor quality, they are still very

In the cutting and shaping process, gems are first cut with a special circular saw, then shaped on a roughly grained carborundum wheel. Transparent stones are first given a rough shape. Then they are faceted (given faces) on a horizontal grinding wheel.

hard. Not good enough to be used as gems, they are called industrial stones, and are still valuable in this form.

Possibly the most interesting use of a gemstone is in the making of a **laser**. This name is formed from the initial letters of the phrase, Light Amplification by Stimulated Emission of Radiation. A ruby crystal is used to produce an intense beam of light, and all of the same **wavelength**. This beam of light can be accurately aimed since it spreads out little. The high energy of a laser beam is used for cutting and melting. Because the wavelength of the light is accurately known, lasers are being used to measure distances with greater accuracy than is possible by any other known method.

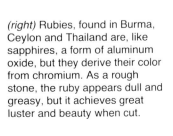

(left) The diamond, shown here in a piece of kimberlite rock, is the hardest of all gems. Diamonds were formed millions of years ago, when carbon from volcanic eruptions cooled slowly under great pressure. Today, deposits are to be found mainly in South Africa and Siberia.

(right) Rubies, found in Burma, Ceylon and Thailand are, like sapphires, a form of aluminum oxide, but they derive their color from chromium. As a rough stone, the ruby appears dull and greasy, but it achieves great luster and beauty when cut.

The earliest life forms

GEOLOGISTS MEASURE TIME in millions of years. Such great lengths of time are very difficult to understand. One way of doing this is to imagine the whole of geological time fitting into a scale covering the twelve months of a year. On this scale the first living cells did not appear until the middle of August, and modern man did not emerge until five minutes before midnight on the very last day of the year.

The way in which geologists describe parts of the geological timescale is to split it into twelve sections, or **periods**. These are given names such as Cambrian, Devonian and Carboniferous. Each era can be recognized by the types of rock and the remains of animals or plants found there. These remains are called fossils.

Several different types of fossil are found buried deep within rocks. The simplest are formed when the dead body of an animal falls into the mud or **silt** of a lake or swamp. The soft parts of the animal gradually rot away to leave the hard bones. These are slowly covered by layers of mud which are dropped, or **deposited**, by rivers. As more and more layers of mud are added, the bottom layers are turned into rock by the pressure of the overlying sediment. Softer animals and plants rot away completely and leave only their shape, or impression, in be-

Rocks are arranged in layers called strata, and the lowest strata are the oldest. The age of a fossil can be estimated from the layer of rock in which it is found. This fossilized fish dates from the Cretaceous period over 100 million years ago.

(below) An artist's reconstruction of the sea bed during the Silurian period. The seas in those times would have contained corals, sea-lilies and trilobites.

January	February	March	April	May	June

tween layers of fine mud or silt. Under certain conditions some animals may have their entire body dissolved away to leave a hollow, or mold, of themselves. Animals that dug burrows, or walked on soft mud, have left evidence of their homes or footprints. These fossils are called trace fossils because they do not actually contain the animal that made them. The footprints of dinosaurs are found in rocks in many parts of the world.

An important part of geology is knowing the age of rocks. The layers of rock can be roughly dated by looking at the types of fossil they contain. A more accurate way of finding the age of rocks is to look for the element carbon in fossils. This substance is the black solid of which coal is

made and is found in all living organisms. When alive, all animals and plants contain carbon, some of which is obtained from the gas, carbon dioxide. This gas is an important part of the Earth's atmosphere.

There are two types of carbon in the air. One type, carbon-14, is **radioactive**; the other is not. The amount, or proportion, of radioactive to ordinary carbon is thought to have been the same throughout geological time. When an animal or plant dies, the carbon it contains includes a known percentage of carbon-14. As with all radioactive atoms, the carbon-14 slowly breaks down, or **decays**, as time passes. This gives us a time-clock built into fossils which helps the scientists to work out age from the

During the Cretaceous period 80 million years ago, the seas were teeming with life. Many of the species, such as cuttlefish and clams, had shells made of calcium carbonate. Their fossilized remains survive as the soft, white rock we call chalk.

percentage of radioactive carbon still left, compared with ordinary carbon.

The earliest known fossils are trace fossils of simple plants called **algae**. These formed deposits of a hard chemical containing calcium, rather like the reefs produced by corals today. The first real fossils did not appear until the Cambrian period, some 500 million years ago. In the seas of that era lived strange organisms called **trilobites**. As with all early fossils their remains are found in rocks formed on the bottom of ancient seas. This world was shared by the first corals and animals called **sea lilies**,

Some scientists believe that the first life forms appeared on Earth over 3 billion years ago. These were the blue-green algae that have been traced in the oldest rocks. If we think of the whole of geological time being squashed into one twelve-month period, the blue-green algae would have appeared in the middle of August. The first dinosaurs would have appeared in mid-November, but Man himself did not appear until five minutes before midnight on the last day of the year.

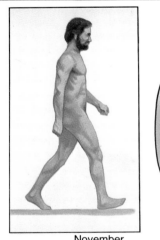

July	August	September	October	November	December

life begins

whose descendants still exist today on the bottom of very deep oceans. In these early seas swam the first relatives of modern squids and cuttlefish which were called **cephalopods** and **ammonites**. All these animals are **invertebrates**, meaning that they have no backbone or skeleton. These first animals produced a whole range of species, some of which are found only at certain times within the fossil record. The fossils are very useful in dating rocks because the organisms from which they were formed existed on Earth for only a short length of time.

The first animals with backbones, called the **vertebrates**, appeared in the early seas of the Ordovician period, some 465 million years ago. They are thought to have resembled eels in

shape but had no real jaw bones. These first fish were covered in bony plates and probably fed upon the dead tissues of plants and animals. By the end of the Devonian period, 340 million years ago, these jawless fish with bony plates had become extinct. They had been replaced by fish with a bony jaw which held sharp teeth. This dramatic change enabled fish to become the most abundant creatures during the Devonian period. They became so common that geologists often called this the 'Age of Fishes'. The development of jaws meant that fish could eat other fish and the numerous invertebrates. This new way of life helped the expansion into new areas, and so set the scene for future animal groups.

- geological time
- first living cells
- Pre-Cambrian
- Cambrian
- Ordovician
- Silurian
- Devonian
- Carboniferous
- Permian
- Triassic
- Jurassic
- Cretaceous
- Tertiary
- Quaternary

Life reaches the land

Until 350 million years ago, life existed only in water. Before this time the land surface would have been a bleak, barren place with no plants to provide food or shelter for animals. By the end of the Devonian period, the dry land had been colonized by the first ferns and horsetails. The fish of that period included a group with strong bony fins. These fish were probably able to drag themselves out of the water. Another very important development was that some of these fish began to breathe air. This meant that they could leave their relatives in the seas and lakes and come on to land. Here, over long periods of time, some of these fish gradually evolved into **amphibian**-like animals. The amphibians living today include frogs, toads and salamanders. They still need water for the growth of their young, or tadpoles. This dependence on water would have restricted the early amphibians to living around the edges of lakes or in swamps.

An important step towards life on land happened when animals were able to carry out their life cycles away from water. The very first large animals to spread over dry land were the reptiles. They had evolved from amphibians during the Carboniferous period, some 300 million years ago. The secret of their success was that they were the first animals to produce shelled eggs. Each egg is like a tiny watery world of its own where the young reptile, or **embryo**, can obtain food and protection without drying out. The reptiles increased in number during the Carboniferous period. In the Triassic period which followed they became as important as the fish had been in the Devonian period. They increased in number and variety until they had occupied much of the land surface.

The Carboniferous period is also important for the large number of plants that flourished in the warm swamps and forests of that age. These died and rotted to create great layers of fossil plants. Through the following 300 million

A scene showing amphibians in swampy land about 300 million years ago (not to scale). The *Ichthyostega* is the earliest known amphibian and was under 1 m long. The *Eogyrinus* was much larger at 5 m long. It led a similar existence to that of present-day alligators and crocodiles. The *Eryops* (1.5 m long) and *Diplocaulus* (60 cm long) are examples of Permian amphibians.

Eryops

Eogyrinus

Diplocaulus

Ichthyostega

years, the **deposits** were buried beneath the sediments of following ages to produce the coal, oil and gas fields which are so important to us today. These deposits of fuel are rich in carbon and have thus given the name of Carboniferous, or 'carbon bearing', to this period of Earth's history.

Meanwhile the reptiles had given rise to a whole range of different groups. One of the earliest groups were the mammal-like reptiles which appear as fossils in rocks of the Permian period. Fossils found in North America and Europe were formed some 270 million years ago. They were the forerunners of the true mammals which developed later in the Earth's history. The most important animals during the next few hundred million years were the dinosaurs. Their fossils have been found in many parts of the world. Some, such as *Brontosaurus*, were plant feeders and may have lived partly in water to help support their enormous bulk. Many dinosaurs, such as *Tyrannosaurus*, were flesh-eaters and preyed upon other dinosaurs. Some reptiles returned to water to eat the numerous fish which still lived there while others took to the air and glided or flew. These flying reptiles are known as pterodactyls.

In fine-grained rocks of southern Germany scientists have found the fossilized skeletons of small animals which had feathered wings. This animal has been given the name *Archeopteryx*, which means 'ancient bird'. The fossil remains are thought to represent an early stage in the development of present-day birds. The development of feathers in *Archeopteryx* was an important step in the evolution of birds because feathers helped them to keep warm. Also, because feathers are light, these early birds were able to fly.

During the invasion of land by amphibians, and then reptiles, another invasion had been going on. Some of the invertebrates from the sea had crawled on to land, probably to feed on the plants. From these first land invertebrates arose the insects. Their success was due to the hard, waterproof skin, or **cuticle**, that helped them to live in the driest of places. Some of the Carboniferous insects included giant dragonflies which flew over the ancient swamps of ferns and horsetails. The remains of these are found in coal deposits.

The period of Earth's history from 350 to 135 million years ago saw the development of reptiles, land plants and land invertebrates. One group which had yet to appear in numbers was the **mammal** group. They were present as very primitive forms from as long ago as 135 million years. They had to wait until the dinosaurs had disappeared before they could begin to come into their own.

A scene during the age of the reptiles, 150 to 200 million years ago. The dinosaurs shown include the *Brontosaurus* (20 m long), *Tyrannosaurus Rex* (6 m high and 15 m long) and the *Iguanadon* (10 m long). Some reptiles, known as pterodactyls, took to the air. The long-tailed *Rhamphorhynchus*, was about the size of a large bird, and the giant *Pterandon*, had a wingspan of 15 m. *Archeopteryx* is regarded as the first feathered bird.

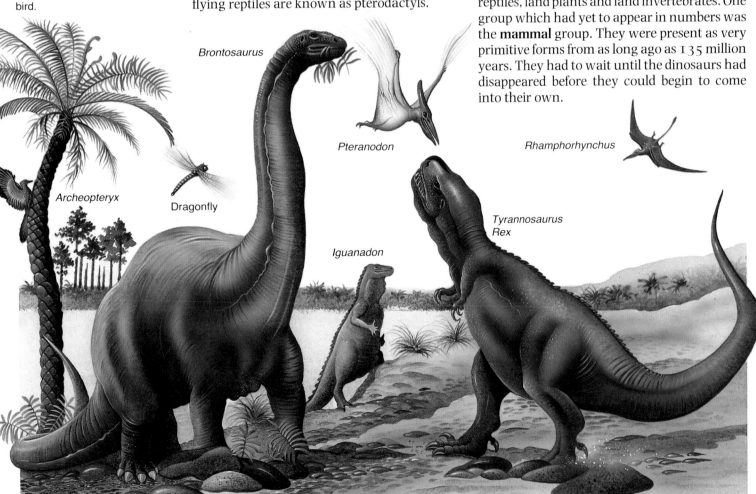

Brontosaurus

Pteranodon

Rhamphorhynchus

Archeopteryx

Dragonfly

Iguanadon

Tyrannosaurus Rex

The age of mammals

AT THE END of the **Cretaceous** period, some 65 million years ago, the great reptiles we call dinosaurs became extinct. The reason why they all died out at about the same time is not really known. We do know that at the end of this period of Earth's history the climate became very cold. This sudden change in climate may have been too much for the dinosaurs to cope with. Whatever the reason, they nearly all disappeared. The crocodiles remained as the only descendants of this once important group.

By the beginning of the Tertiary era, the continents were much as we know them today. Africa had split from South America, and India was part of Asia. By that time the early mammals had already divided into two main groups. The **marsupials**, which now include the kangaroo and koala bear, survived in Australia, New Zealand and parts of South America. The rest of present-day mammals are called **placental** mammals and are found all over Africa, Europe, Asia, North and South America. Both these groups of mammals have evolved in

climates and landscapes similar to those we now see on Earth.

The vast numbers of mammals which we find today are living proof of their success, but this has only been possible because of the extinction of competitors, such as the dinosaurs. Like these, there have been many large mammals which have died out during the past 60 million years or so. The climate of Earth has undergone many changes since that time. The cold periods that may have killed off the dinosaurs have been repeated many times.

One of the features of mammals is that they are covered in hair or fur and this helps them to keep warm. All mammals are warm-blooded, which means that they carefully control their own body temperature. By doing this they can live in places which are much too cold for other animals. The great majority of animals which live in the cold polar regions are mammals. The thick fur of the polar bear and arctic fox help

The early mammals had divided into two main groups by the beginning of the Tertiary era: the marsupials and the placental mammals. There are about 170 species of Australasian marsupials, which include the Goodfellow's tree kangaroo, the red kangaroo, the sugar glider, a type of flying squirrel, and the koala.

them to keep out the freezing cold and keep in their own body heat.

During the last two million years, at least four major ice ages have occurred. During each ice age much of the Northern Hemisphere was covered in sheets of ice and snow. The mammals that lived in these regions had to **adapt** to the cold conditions or become extinct. Since these mammals lived fairly recently, in terms of geological time, they have left many good fossils. From these remains we have been able to discover the many types of mammals which lived during that time. The main feature of most of the mammals was their long hair. Hairy elephants, or mammoths, once roamed over much of northern Europe, Asia and America. Their bones have been found in caves and rocks throughout these regions. Complete deep-frozen mammoths have been dug out of ice-sheets in parts of Siberia.

Many of the ancient mammals were larger than those we find today. Saber-toothed tigers roamed the Earth alongside huge bears and woolly rhinoceroses. They were hunted by the most dangerous of all mammals, the human animal. Our ancestors developed from the first apes on the plains of Africa, some 30 million years ago. It took a further 28 million years before the first real human animals appeared on Earth. In the last great ice age, a mere 100,000 years ago, an ancestor of the modern human roamed the cold forests of northern Europe and Asia. Scientists have given this ancestor the name **Neanderthal** man. The large numbers of fossils left behind have helped us to discover quite a lot about the way he lived. Tools and weapons have been found next to the fossilized bones of the animals Neanderthal man killed and ate. Many of these animals include types now extinct.

Most early mammals had to adapt to the harsh conditions of the ice ages. Both the mammoth, a type of elephant, and the rhinoceros had thick, woolly coats and powerful tusks and horns. The large cats had long, saber-like teeth which they used as efficient weapons to kill the thick-skinned animals on which they preyed.

Evidence of animals long extinct is found in fossils. These are *Diplodocus* bones at the Dinosaur National Monument in Utah, USA.

Much effort has been put into tracing human ancestry. The only evidence we have is the fossilized remains. These are rare, mainly because the species itself was probably rare. Once dead the body of Neanderthal man would have been eaten by wild animals, and the bones scattered far and wide. In trying to fit together the pieces of human **evolution**, the careful dating of the remains of our ancestors has been very important. Despite all these difficulties we probably know more about the origin of the human animal than of any other animal group. All this knowledge is based upon fossils.

Ice ages and glaciers

AT THE NORTH AND SOUTH POLES we find huge sheets of ice and snow. Those at the North Pole lie over an ocean and extend into northern Canada, Europe and Greenland. The continent of Antarctica, on which lies the South Pole, is covered by a sheet of ice which is called an **ice-cap**. During the winter in polar regions, the air is so cold that any water which falls from clouds is quickly frozen into crystals of ice that we call snow. Unlike other parts of the world where snow falls, the polar summers are too short and cold for all the snow to melt.

Over millions of years the soft, fluffy snow has built up into deep layers where the weight of the upper layers turns the bottom ones into rock-hard ice. The weight of ice makes the **ice-sheet** act as if it were a liquid, and so flow downhill. In mountainous regions the ice flows down valleys as rivers of ice called **glaciers**. These can move at various speeds from a few centimeters to as much as 200 m per year.

During the course of Earth's history, there have been several periods when the polar ice-caps have increased to cover surrounding continents. Such periods are called ice ages. Exactly why they occur is not fully understood, but they happen when the climate of the Earth gets cooler. The last great ice age began about 18,000 years ago when much of Europe was held in the grip of glaciers and **snow-fields**. In the geological timescale this last ice age took place so recently that we are still recovering

The Alps have some 1300 glaciers. Most glaciers are slow-moving, and it may take one hundred years for a piece of ice to move from the head to the foot of an Alpine glacier.

The rock material carried down by the ice-sheet to the foot or sides of a glacier is called moraine. The photograph shows a moraine in the Vitosha mountains, in Bulgaria.

from it. We know quite a lot about the timing and extent of these ice ages because of the evidence they left on rocks and the landscape.

As ice moves downhill, it picks up fragments of rock which are broken away from the solid rock above and below the ice. The fragments either fall into cracks, or **crevasses**, in the ice, or stick into the underneath of the glacier or ice-sheet. These rock fragments give the ice a very rough surface, just like sandpaper on a very large scale. With this cutting-edge of rock fragments, ice can wear away even the hardest rocks. The **bedrock** over which the ice flows is smoothed down and left with an almost polished surface. The direction in which the ice moved is shown by scratches and grooves which were caused by the sharp edges of rock fragments as they moved over the bedrock. In mountainous regions glaciers build up in existing valleys. The rock in the bottom of these valleys is then gradually ground away by the movement of the glaciers. Such valleys, along which glaciers have passed, are clearly U-shaped while those created by rivers are V-shaped in cross-section.

The evidence of ice ages is seen in mountainous areas throughout the world. The Alps, in Europe, and the Southern Alps, in New Zealand, are both examples of areas affected by

dumped by the ice, while clay and sand are washed many miles away.

Many glaciers do not end on land. Some flow into the sea, where chunks break off to form icebergs. When the seas around the Poles freeze every winter they extend the ice-cap with a fringe of sea-ice. This is slowly broken up as summer approaches and forms pack-ice which is carried away by ocean currents until it gradually melts.

At the height of the ice ages, much of the sea-ice formed did not melt. Instead, it added to the weight of ice over the land. As we now know, the continents are really enormous blocks of rock floating on a liquid layer of molten rock deep within the Earth. As the ice built up during the ice ages, the weight caused the land to sink.

recent ice ages. Less obvious evidence of ice ages is found in the huge amounts of gravel, rock, clay and sand that have been moved by glaciers and ice-sheets. This mixture of powdered rock and boulders is called **moraine**. It is either pushed forward by an advancing glacier, or left behind when it melts. The point where a glacier stops growing is marked by a ridge, or **terminal moraine**. The melting ice leaves small cone-shaped piles of rock debris called drumlins. Much of North America is today covered in the moraine left by glaciers and ice-sheets. This has been moved since the last ice age by the action of running water to form an **outwash plain**. The heavy boulders are left where they were

(right) The Matterhorn, in the Alps, shows the results of prolonged glacial activity.

(below) The extent of ice coverage in the last ice age, 18,000 years ago, is shown below, by the red line. The dotted line shows the polar and Greenland ice-cap as it is today.

A glacier is a slow-moving river of ice. Cracks, called crevasses, appear on the surface due to the great pressures. Rocks transported by the ice-sheet are called moraine. As a glacier recedes, a U-shaped valley is left containing moraine material deposited by the glacier at an earlier time.

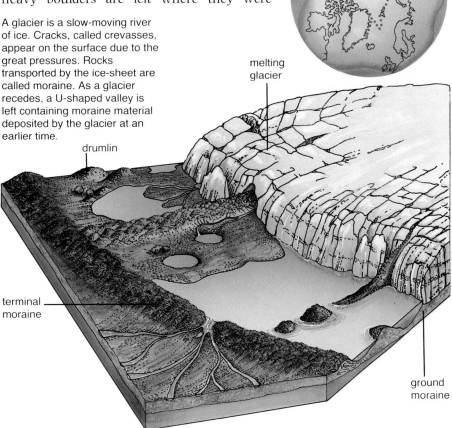

drumlin

melting glacier

terminal moraine

ground moraine

As the climate warmed up, and the ice retreated back to the polar regions, two things happened. Firstly the melting ice raised the sea-level. Secondly, the removal of the weight of ice meant that the continents began to rise again. The process of land rising, or **uplift**, is still happening today. It can be seen on the coasts of northern Europe where old beaches are now dry land.

Thus the ice ages were times of great change in the landscape with land rising and falling. The effect on living things was to keep them moving south as the ice advanced and north as the ice retreated. These movements are recorded in the fossils of animals which were left in the moraines and in the deposits associated with each ice age.

Change and erosion

THE SURFACE of our world is changing and has been doing so since the Earth was formed millions of years ago. Mountains have been lifted up and worn away, and yet more mountains have risen in their place. The process of rocks being pushed upwards, broken down and deposited on the bottom of oceans and lakes goes on all the time.

The rocks we find on the surface of the Earth are of three types. The first are the **igneous** rocks, meaning 'born of fire' because they are thrust from deep within the Earth and emerge at the surface in volcanoes. These rocks are made from crystals of the molten minerals which exist deep within the Earth.

The second type, the **metamorphic** rocks, are also hard, resistant rocks. This name means that they have 'changed shape' because of the high pressures and temperatures deep within the crust. They include small crystals but have never actually been melted.

The final type, the sedimentary rocks, are formed from the particles of other rocks which have been broken off, or eroded. **Erosion** is brought about by the action of water, ice, wind or chemicals. These particles are carried in rivers and dropped as mud, sand or silt in lakes and seas. The pressure deep within layers of such sediment begins the process of rock formation. Some sedimentary rocks are made from the dead bodies of microscopic sea animals. The white cliffs of Dover, facing the English Channel, consist of chalk which is a soft rock made from microscopic shells of sea organisms called **foraminifera** and **radiolaria**.

A cave with stalactites (hanging) and stalagmites (standing) caused by chemicals in rain water acting on limestone.

Erosion of the Earth's surface is caused by many forces. The effects of gravity, ice, frost, rain, rivers, waves, wind and chemicals all contribute to the eventual formation of sedimentary rocks in the sea. As these are uplifted they in turn are worn away in the continuous erosion process.

All these rock types are likely to be broken down, or eroded, once they are exposed to weather. The process of erosion is a part of the natural cycle which builds up and breaks down landscapes. Once the rock has been broken into fragments or particles, these are transported from their 'parent' rock to the place where they are deposited as sediment. The most common way this happens is when water picks up the particles. Winds can also transport fine grains of sand and dust. Rock fragments, carried by glaciers, can travel hundreds of kilometers before settling on river beds.

Most rocks are very hard, and geologists need to use heavy hammers to break pieces off. The process of erosion begins with the exposure of rocks to the climate, a process known as weathering. This means that the rock is weakened by constant heating and cooling, or by the freezing of water which seeps into cracks in the rock. These processes gradually cause pieces of rock to flake away. Many rocks are affected by the gases dissolved in rainwater. This is chemical weathering and is caused mainly by the gas carbon dioxide, which dissolves in water to form a weak acid.

A type of sedimentary rock called limestone is easily weathered by water containing carbon dioxide. Limestone is broken down by the acid and the chemicals produced dissolve in the water to form a solution. This solution trickles through cracks in the rock to form underground caves and streams. As it slowly seeps through the cave roofs, some of the water from

chemical weathering this is broken down into soft **china clay**, used to make china pottery.

Once the rock has been weathered, it can then be worn away by rain or water in streams. Running water wears away rocks by the constant movement, or friction, of gravel and particles of sand carried by the current. Rivers are always wearing away their beds and they create deep valleys. The deepest valleys, or gorges, in the world have been formed because of the constant erosion by rivers. The Grand Canyon, in Arizona, is 1824 meters deep and has been carved out by the flow of the Colorado River.

In dry parts of the world, erosion by water is a rare event. In desert regions the occasional rain storms scour out deep, straight-sided gorges called **wadis**. However, for most of the time, the desert landscape is shaped by a different process. The strong winds which travel across the hot deserts pick up particles of dust and sand. These grains are very hard and rough. Indeed, we use sand blasting to clean up

the solution evaporates. This causes some of the dissolved limestone to become solid again to form icicle-shaped lumps of rock called **stalactites**. Underneath these, drips fall to build up pointed cones called **stalagmites**.

A similar weathering process affects granite, an extremely hard rock. Under the influence of

An arch formed by wave erosion of a coastal headland.

(right) Persistent sandblasting by the wind has caused this desert feature.

In very dry regions flash-floods caused by the rare torrential rains can lead to severe erosion. Over the years steep-sided ravines, or wadis, are formed.

buildings in our cities. The erosion caused by the wind-borne sand grains has created a very special type of landscape in deserts. Outcrops of rock are constantly blasted by the grains and smoothed into rounded shapes.

The real power of water as a force which causes erosion is seen around the coasts of continents. Powerful waves bombard the shore and cliffs with a barrage of shingle. The more resistant, or harder, rocks form headlands, while softer rocks are worn away to create bays. Evidence of erosion by the sea is seen everywhere along the seashore. Huge boulders that have been broken off cliffs lie at the top of the beach, and the finely powdered rock which makes sand is moved along the coast. The sea does not have it all its own way. Where rivers enter the sea they drop their sediment and create **deltas** of sediment which over thousands of years push back the sea and form new land.

Earthquakes

AN EARTHQUAKE is the name given to a violent heaving and shaking of the ground. Great cracks may open in the earth, and buildings may be shaken so severely that they crack and fall down. Normally, the shaking lasts for

The great Alaska earthquake was one of the largest ever recorded and caused immense building damage *(left)*. However, because it affected such a sparsely populated area few lives were lost relative to the shock, which caused a permanent tilting of the land along Alaska's southern coast.

The effects of a sideways shift in the ground, known as a lateral fault, photographed in a field in California

less than a minute. The Great Alaska earthquake of 1964 started without warning, as a gentle, rolling movement, followed by over three minutes of hard shaking. This then gradually subsided. Following the main earthquake, smaller quakes called **aftershocks** continued for several hours. Very minor quakes continued for a further nine months.

About a million earthquakes happen each year. Fortunately, only a few are strong enough to cause severe damage and loss of life. The majority of earthquakes are not powerful enough to be felt. Their existence is known only to scientists. They study earthquakes, using sensitive instruments called **seismographs**.

It is not only the earthquakes which can cause damage. Some have been known to set off tremendous landslides and giant sea waves, which have wrecked entire cities. The giant sea waves are called **tsunamis**. They are produced by a sudden movement of the sea bed. This might result either from a volcanic explosion under water, or from a major earthquake. It is not necessarily the largest earthquakes which cause the greatest damage. An earthquake can create great destruction and loss of life if it severely rocks the ground in a densely popu-

lated area, where buildings are not specifically built to withstand earthquakes. Where old houses are built on poor soil, damage may be particularly severe. The earthquake in Southern Italy, on 23rd November 1980, killed 3000 people and left 300,000 homeless.

Nearly all earthquakes occur in areas where there are cracks in the Earth's crust. These cracks, known as faults, are mainly situated near the edges of the plates in the crust, which support the continents and ocean basins. On either side of a fault, the rock of the crust may move against the rock on the other side. This movement may be up, down or sideways. For many years, the rocks on each side of the fault slide slowly and steadily past each other. Suddenly, both sides jam solid. Tremendous pressures, called stresses, build up and the rocks bend very slightly. It is like winding up a huge clock-spring. At last, the stresses in the rocks become stronger than the bond which is holding the blocks of rock together. The rocks on each side of the fault move with a sudden jolt,

As pressures build up between rock masses along a fault line (a) the rocks begin to buckle (b). Eventually the stresses become so great (c) that the friction between the two is overcome and movement occurs. The rocks adjust to new positions to relieve the strain (d). Harry Reid, an American, was the first to put forward this theory after the 1906 San Francisco earthquake and called it 'elastic rebound'.

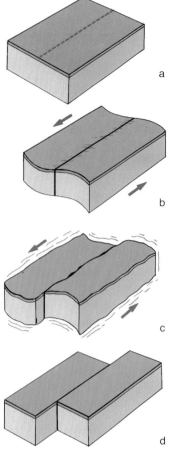

a

b

c

d

like the unwinding of a coiled clock-spring when suddenly released. The place where the sudden jolt occurs is called the **focus** of the earthquake.

Now that the stress is relieved, the rocks spring back to their normal shape. From the focus, vibrations spread out in all directions through the surrounding rocks. These vibrations are called seismic waves. They are felt, at ground level, as the violent shaking of an earthquake. Smaller vibrations, the aftershocks, will continue until the rocks have settled down.

Seismic waves may be recorded, using a seismograph. The most sensitive can magnify the shaking of the ground a million times. In a modern seismograph, a very heavy pendulum is supported on a frame. This is arranged in such a way that, although the frame shakes in an earthquake, the massive pendulum does not move. A long arm with a pen at the end leads from the pendulum to a rotating drum, over which lies a long roll of paper. The drum shakes in the earthquake, but the arm and pen remain

appear on the seismogram are the primary, or P waves. These travel through the crust at 5 km per second. Later, on the seismogram, a stronger and more ragged tracing appears. This marks the arrival of the secondary, or S waves. These travel through the crust at 3 km per second.

The tracings on a seismogram tell scientists much about the earthquake which caused them. They can tell precisely where it occurred and how far the focus was below the Earth's surface. The place on the surface directly above the focus is called the **epicenter** of the earthquake. Normally, severe earthquakes are commonly known by the name of the place nearest to the epicenter. This is where most damage and human suffering occurs. Seismograms may also be used to tell how powerful an earthquake was, and in which direction the ground shifted.

Scientists have set up special seismic observatories all over the world. In each, different types of seismograph are used to record the different types of wave. To fix the position of an epicenter, readings from at least three observatories are needed. P waves travel faster than S waves. Because of this, the time interval which elapses between the arrival of the P and S waves increases with distance from the epicenter. By measuring this time interval accurately, seismologists can determine the distance of the epicenter from each observatory.

An off-shore earthquake caused an avalanche from the Peruvian mountain Nevados Husascaran in 1970. The avalanche fell 4000 m burying the town of Yungay under rock debris 10 m deep and caused thousands of deaths. The pictures show the mountain before and after the avalanche.

still. The result is a wiggly line on the paper. This record on paper is called a seismogram.

When an earthquake occurs, seismic waves spread out from the focus at different speeds. If these waves are recorded by a seismograph, some distance away, three different types of wave may be identified. The first waves to

Volcanoes

Molten magma develops deep down inside the Earth in the lower part of the crust and in the upper parts of the mantle, as a result of movement between the two. Where the crust is weak the magma forces its way upwards until it eventually reaches the surface.

WHEN A VOLCANO ERUPTS, we see the tremendous forces which are at work beneath the Earth's surface. If we could travel towards the center of the Earth, we would find that the temperature rises, reaching a value of about 4000°C at the center. In spite of these very high temperatures, much of the Earth is solid. This is because the pressure compressing the rock also increases with depth. Where the lower part of the Earth's crust joins the upper part of the mantle, the temperature is high enough and the pressure just low enough for some rock to melt. The molten rock is called magma.

Often the magma collects into large underground chambers called **magma reservoirs**. Magma is a mixture of molten rock and bubbles of gas. The magma in the reservoirs tries continually to rise up towards the surface. Sometimes, the magma may break through a crack in the Earth's crust and pour out on to the surface, causing a volcanic eruption.

As a volcano erupts, the pressure on the magma drops suddenly. The magma bubbles and fizzes as the gas is given off. The faster the gas escapes, the more violent is the volcanic eruption. If the molten rock is very liquid, the gas escapes easily and the volcano erupts gently. If it is thick, the gas has to force its way out and this can produce a violent explosion. Most volcanoes also pour out molten rock as well as gas. The molten rock flowing out of a volcano is called lava. It is very hot, having a temperature of 900°C to 1200°C. As the lava cools, it becomes solid and the volcano builds up. If the lava is very liquid it flows out rapidly and floods over the land, forming a flattish area of rock. If the lava is slightly thicker, a low volcanic cone forms. Very thick lava does not flow far during an eruption. It tends to pile up close to the mouth or **vent** of the volcano, forming a steep-sided cone.

A volcano may produce thick lava during one eruption, and liquid lava at another. If there has been a long gap between eruptions, the lava is normally thick and the eruption more violent. In an explosive eruption, pieces of rock of all sizes may be thrown out. The smallest particles are volcanic ash and are less than 4 mm across. Fragments between 4 mm and 32 mm in diameter are called **lapilli**, which means 'little stones' in Latin. Larger fragments are called volcanic bombs if they are molten, or blocks if they are solid. The smaller pieces will travel the furthest from the site of the eruption. Volcanic

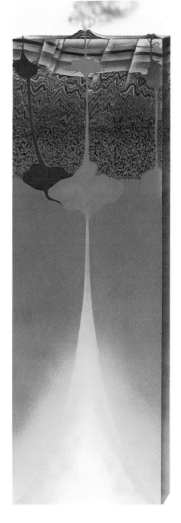

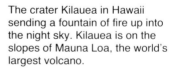

The crater Kilauea in Hawaii sending a fountain of fire up into the night sky. Kilauea is on the slopes of Mauna Loa, the world's largest volcano.

(right) Lady Knox geyser, New Zealand. Sometimes the hot magma underground does not erupt. Instead the hot gas seeps out through cracks in the crust and heats up water in rock near the surface. This can produce geysers, hot springs and bubbling mud pools. Geysers shoot jets of boiling water and steam high into the air.

ash may be thrown high into the atmosphere and can have a great effect on the world's weather for long periods.

Volcanic eruptions are given different names, depending on how violent they are. Hawaiian eruptions are the quietest of all. The lava is very liquid, and the gas escapes easily. Kilauea, in Hawaii, is an example of this type of volcano. Strombolian eruptions are a little more violent. The lava is less liquid, and every few minutes there is a small explosion. The eruptions are named after the island of Stromboli off the coast of Italy. Vulcanian eruptions are more violent still. The lava is fairly thick, and the gas forcing its way out causes a series of explosions. Parts of the volcanic cone itself may be blown away and large amounts of solid blocks and volcanic ash are thrown into the air. In a Vesuvian eruption there is often a continuous explosive blast which may last for several hours. Many more fragments are blown out of the volcano, and the plume of gas and fine ash will rise high into the atmosphere. This type of eruption is named after Mount Vesuvius, near Naples in Italy, which erupted violently on 24th August in the year AD 79, burying the two towns of Pompeii and Herculaneum.

Plinian eruptions are the most violent of all. They take their name from the Roman writer Pliny the Younger, who described the AD 79 eruption of Vesuvius in great detail. In Plinian eruptions, the explosion is so devastating that

It is sometimes very difficult to say whether a volcano is extinct or dormant. In 1973, scientists, as well as the rest of the world, were very surprised when the volcano Helgafell in Iceland erupted. It had been dormant for 5000 years.

the volcano is almost completely destroyed. On 27th August, 1883, the island of Krakatoa, between Sumatra and Java, in Indonesia, suffered such a fate. The explosion was heard nearly 4800 km away, as the 'roar of heavy guns'. Another type of eruption is the Peléean type. Here, the lava is very thick and solidifies into a volcanic plug which blocks the vent of the volcano. The plug can only be removed by a violent gas explosion, which forms a glowing cloud of hot volcanic gas and ash. The glowing cloud produced by the eruption of Mount Pelée in 1902 killed 30,000 people on the island of Martinique.

There are some 530 active volcanoes on Earth, of which about 80 are under the sea. Only a few of these are erupting at any one time, perhaps about 25 per year. Several, like Stromboli, are erupting more or less continually. Between eruptions, a volcano is said to be dormant (sleeping). A volcano may be dormant for a few years or for thousands of years. An extinct (or dead) volcano is one that has not erupted for so long that scientists think it will never erupt again.

A truly dramatic story is that of Mount St Helens in Washington State. In March 1980 danger signals were observed and scientists gathered a mass of instruments to record the predicted volcanic activity. On Sunday, 18th May, the bulging north wall of the mountain fell off with a blast that could be heard up to 480 km away and had the force of a major nuclear explosion. Winds of more than 1250 kph were recorded and for nearly two days there rose up millions of tons of ash which spread over the Atlantic into Europe. It was only several months later that a plug of lava grew big enough to seal the vent.

The Earth seen from space

THE FIRST artificial **satellite** to be put into orbit around the Earth was Sputnik 1, launched by the Russians on 4th October, 1957. Explorer 1, the first American satellite, followed on 31st January, 1958. The earliest satellites were simply constructed and carried few instruments. It was only in 1960 that the first satellites to carry cameras were launched. These cameras could show no features on the Earth smaller than about 2 square kilometers, but since then the quality has greatly improved. Maybe by the year 2000 it will be possible to see objects as small as a meter across, from orbits nearly 1000 km above the Earth's surface. However, this accuracy will be limited, not by the quality of the camera on the satellite, but by the turbulence of the Earth's atmosphere through which the camera must look.

In the mid-1960s, people began to realize that there was a need to obtain accurate information on the world's shrinking resources. These include forests, minerals, and fossil fuels, such as coal and oil. The American space administration, NASA, decided to develop a series of satellites which could orbit the Earth and observe its surface continuously with high quality cameras. These satellites became known as Earth Resources Satellites. The first of these was launched on 23rd July, 1972 and was called the Earth Research Technology

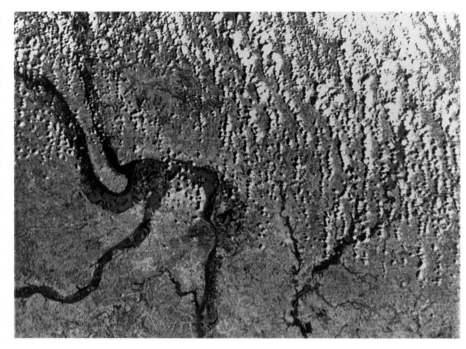

These two Landsat photographs, taken at different times, show St Louis and the Mississippi/Missouri river system at normal and at flood levels. On this occasion the river was 11 m above normal level and vast flood damage took place.

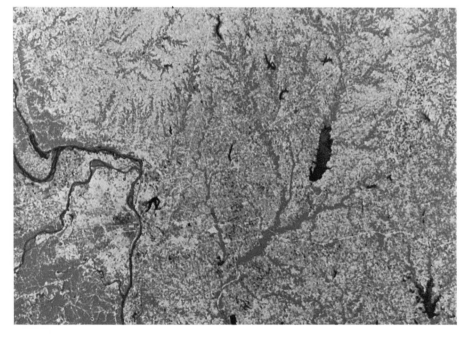

Satellite, or ERTS-1 for short. It continued working for seven years. Later satellites in this series have been known simply as Landsat-2, Landsat-3 and so on. Landsat-2 was launched in January 1975, and Landsat-3 in March 1978. These satellites were capable of photographing details on the Earth's surface as small as 60 square meters.

The cameras used on each Landsat satellite are extremely complex. They use a process called **remote sensing**, in which the cameras scan the Earth to look for different patterns of radiation. The Landsat cameras view the Earth both in visible light, which can be seen by the human eye, and also in infrared light, a form of radiation that cannot be seen by the human eye. When infrared radiation falls on the skin it gives a sensation of warmth. It is sometimes called heat or **thermal radiation**. A single Landsat picture taken from a height of about 900 km shows a ground area of some 35,000 square kilometers. Each satellite can take pictures of the daylight side of the Earth's globe, every day throughout the year. Landsat pictures are converted into a stream of electrical pulses and beamed down from the satellite to Earth.

Computer centers on the ground use special techniques to translate the data received from

Landsat into **false-color pictures**. These use different colors to show variation in the visible light, or infrared radiation picked up by the satellite camera. By studying these false-color pictures, scientists are able to make many interesting observations. They have been used for many applications, to assist oceanographers, geologists, foresters and many others in their work. They enable observers to follow the movement of the ice-caps near the Poles and of the sand dunes of the desert. The flow of water in the rivers and oceans may also be observed. The annual flooding of the world's great rivers such as the Nile and Ganges are vital to millions of people. Satellite photographs show these events in minute detail, including the movement of the enormous amount of sediment that these rivers leave behind.

The San Andreas fault *(above)* stretches over 400 km from San Francisco. It runs diagonally across the picture from bottom right to top left.

Venice, Italy, photographed from Skylab 2, is built on almost 120 islands. These are linked by bridges and criss-crossed by canals, which are the city's roads.

False color image of the Italian coastline near Rome, taken from Landsat 1, in February 1973. In this picture, nearly 200 km of coastline is shown. Rome itself is the pale blue patch half-way up and 2 cm from the left edge of the picture.

The infrared satellite photographs are very useful, particularly for showing areas of diseased and healthy vegetation. Healthy plants appear red, because they strongly reflect infrared light. The exact tone of the red indicates how old the plants are. Young plants show bright red while those ready for harvesting appear dark red. Plants affected by drought and disease can be identified by the different color of their images compared with the dark red of healthy vegetation. Satellite photographs are also useful to the environmental scientists, enabling major sources of pollution in both the air and water to be observed. Deep, clear water appears perfectly black, but polluted water shows as faint grey-green haze in the image. Human effects on the environment can be clearly seen from the satellite photographs. In addition to keeping a close eye on the environment, the images provide vital information on the efficiency of agricultural methods, use of the land, and the health of all growing crops.

Recent developments in Earth Resources spacecraft include the new Landsat-D satellite, which can obtain pictures showing detail as small as only 30 m. By the late-1980s, satellites which will give color pictures showing features as small as 20 m, and black-and-white images at only 10 m, will be a realistic possibility. A number of SEASAT satellites are also being launched in the mid-1980s, to examine the resources of the oceans and the properties of major river estuaries. They will also monitor waterborne pollution. Complex computers linked to these satellites will give drought warnings and flood alerts.

The Earth's atmosphere and winds

THE EARTH is enclosed inside a fairly thin blanket of air called the atmosphere. The gases that make up the atmosphere are held close to our planet by the force of the Earth's gravity. The atmosphere acts as a protective shield between life on the Earth's surface and cold, hostile space. Seen from space, Earth is partly hidden by swirling masses of cloud. These are found only in the lower parts of the atmosphere, called the **troposphere**. This quite shallow band of air, extending up to about 15 km above the ground, is very important. In this layer are found all the gases essential for life, including water vapor and water droplets, or clouds. Above the troposphere, the atmosphere consists of thinned-out gases. This layer, the **stratosphere** reaches to a height of about 50 km.

The millions upon millions of gas molecules in the atmosphere press down on each other to cause a pressure called air pressure. If we travel up a mountain or in a balloon, we would find that the air pressure gets less the higher we go. This effect can be compared to a pile of blankets

The atmosphere is made up of three main layers, the troposphere, stratosphere and ionosphere. These are separated by the dividing layers, the tropopause and stratopause. Contained within the stratosphere is the ozone layer or ozonosphere. The troposphere holds 90 per cent of the entire air mass, although it only reaches a height of 15,000 m. The upper layers are made up of much thinner gases which stay at regular temperatures. Above the stratosphere, the gases in the ionosphere are electrically charged.

Balloons need to be lighter than air to fly. Some use the gas helium but the use of hot air is more common. Once aloft the pilot uses burners to keep the air hot inside the balloon's envelope. If the air cools the balloon will sink back to Earth.

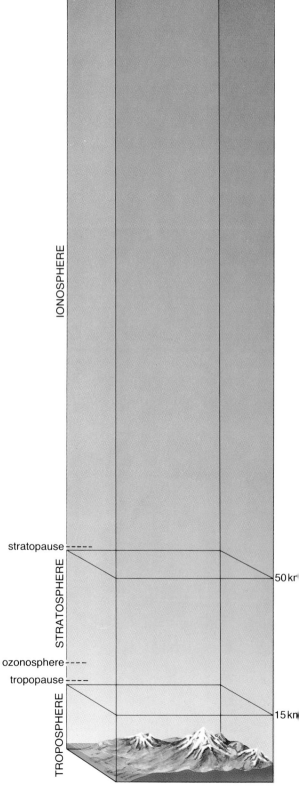

on your bed. A single blanket feels very light, while many blankets feel heavy on your body. In exactly the same way, the layers of air in the atmosphere press down on the layers below. This means that the greatest air pressure is found at ground level. Further out in the stratosphere the air pressure falls to almost zero because there is hardly any air above it. Once space itself is reached, air pressure does not exist as space contains no air or gases of any kind. Airliners that fly in the stratosphere have pressurized cabins to enable us to breathe at those heights.

The pressure of the atmosphere at ground level is not the same throughout the world. As the Sun's rays travel through the atmosphere they pass on little of their heat to the air. Once they strike the land and sea they pass on most of their heat to the rocks, soil and water. These in turn heat the air above them. One of the properties of air is that warm air is lighter than cold air. This means that as the air above the ground is heated it rises up into the atmosphere. As the warm air rises it leaves behind an area of **low pressure** because the air has been made lighter by heating and does not 'press' so heavily on the

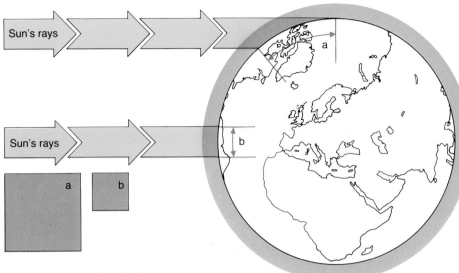

A comparison showing that the Sun's rays at the equator are more concentrated than they are elsewhere. They have far less atmosphere to pass through than they do at the poles. Because of this, they are much weaker at the poles and the land never heats up.

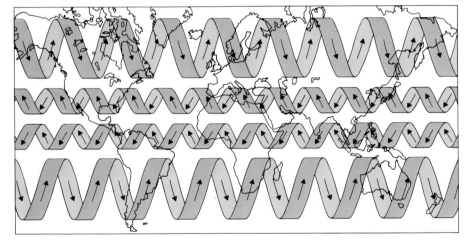

ground. Around the equator, where the Sun's rays are strongest, a band of low pressure is always present.

At the Poles the Sun's rays are very weak, and as a result the land is cold and the sea frozen. The air above these regions is being constantly cooled and sinks towards the ground. This sinking, or heavy air causes permanent **high pressure** areas over the North and South Poles.

At the equator the rising air spreads out north and south. At the Poles the sinking air spreads out along the lower regions of the atmosphere. The two movements of air create further bands of high or low pressure in between the equator and Poles.

A wind is named by the direction from which it comes. Thus a north wind blows from the north. The major winds of the world are the Westerlies (top and bottom) and the Trade winds (center). The rotation of the Earth causes them to move with a spiral effect.

The areas of high and low pressure are constantly trying to even out. Any gas at high pressure tries to move into an area of low pressure. This is easily seen when you press the nozzle of an aerosol spray. A gas is held at high pressure inside the can and escapes as a 'wind' to the outside when we create a gap by pressing the nozzle. The winds which blow in every part of the world are caused by the areas of high and low pressure in our atmosphere. In the aerosol spray the 'wind' shoots out in a straight line between the high pressure within the can and the lower pressure outside. Winds that blow over the Earth do not blow in straight lines between high and low pressures. They are bent by the movement of the Earth itself. As the world turns, winds are pushed to the right in the Northern Hemisphere and to the left in the Southern Hemisphere. The pushing is called the **Coriolis effect**.

In the past, when ships relied upon wind to fill their sails, sailors gave names to some regular winds. For example, the strong winds that blow towards the equator are still known as the 'trade winds'. Just as important to sailors were those parts of the ocean where no winds blew. Here, the sailing ships could not move, or were becalmed. An example of this is the band of low pressure around the equator called the Doldrums. Another area of calm air, called the horse latitudes, exists in a band of high pressure across the Northern Hemisphere. This name was given by the Spanish sailors who were taking horses across to Spain's American colonies. Once the ship was becalmed, the horses often ran out of food and water. To lighten the ship and help it to catch every breeze, the sailors killed the horses and threw them overboard.

The water cycle

ALL THROUGH THE YEAR, the rays of the Sun heat the land and the sea. When water is warmed by the Sun's rays, some of it turns into an invisible gas, or vapor. This water vapor mixes with all the other gases that combine to form air.

Water makes up more than three-quarters of most living organisms, and life cannot exist without it. Plants take in water, and most of this is given out by **evaporation** from the leaves. This process, called **transpiration**, is continually adding a large amount of water vapor to the Earth's atmosphere.

Warm air can hold much more water vapor than cold air. As air is warmed over land and sea, it absorbs water vapor. The moist air then rises in the atmosphere and begins to cool. In cooling, the air is less able to mix with water vapor. Some of this water vapor condenses into very small droplets of water. These droplets collect together in the atmosphere to form clouds.

Winds in the atmosphere cause the clouds to move into patches of warmer or colder air. If a newly formed cloud is warmed, some of the water droplets will turn back into water vapor and the cloud will get smaller. If the cloud is cooled still further, extra water will condense on to the tiny droplets and they will become rain-

drops. When clouds form over oceans they are usually driven by winds until they meet a mountain or high ground on land. Here they are forced upward by currents of air and in doing so are cooled down. This is why the coastal slopes of mountains often have heavy rainfall.

For exactly the opposite reasons the other side of those mountains is usually dry because clouds are descending into warmer air. As this happens, some of the water droplets turn back into vapor, the clouds become smaller and the rain stops. This part of the mountain is called a **rain shadow**. When rain falls over the mountain it collects in tiny streams and eventually

In the cold morning air, dew may form on grass, trees and even spiders' webs. Water vapor in the air condenses into water droplets when the temperature falls to a point known as the dew point. As the air warms up again, the droplets evaporate.

The cycle of water *(below)*. Heat from the Sun evaporates the water from the sea and land. The water rises up into the air as vapor and forms clouds. The vapor condenses and falls to Earth as rain, snow and hail. Some of it flows back into the sea.

runs into rivers and the sea. So we see that water follows a cycle, starting with evaporation from land and sea. This water vapor forms clouds, and in due course the water returns to the Earth's surface as rain. The cycle is then repeated over and over again.

Clouds form when moist, warm air meets cold air. The way clouds form, and the temperatures to which they fall, will affect their shape and the type of 'rain'. If the rain cloud is quickly swept upward into freezing air, the rain droplets will turn into pellets of ice called hailstones. If the cloud is very cold before the droplets are large enough to form hailstones, the water freezes into ice crystals, or snow. When the air over the ground is cold, mist can produce ice crystals, or frost, on the ground.

The land and sea are heated by the Sun during daytime, and warm up at different speeds. The land heats up quickly but only to a depth of 40 cm or so. The sea heats up slowly because the hot surface layers are mixed with the cooler layers beneath. At night, as the land and sea cool down, the opposite happens. The land cools much more quickly for the same reasons it heated up quickly during the day. The seas cool slowly, in fact about two and one-half times slower than land. As a result, land and sea are at different temperatures during the day and night. In the daytime the land is much warmer

almost opposite directions from one season to another. In winter, dry winds blow across India from the cold land masses in the north, the Himalayas and southern Siberia. In summer, the Indian land mass heats up rapidly. The monsoon blows off the sea from the southeast, bringing with it violent thunderstorms and heavy, continuous rainfall over a period of a few weeks.

Rainstorm as the Sun goes down over the North Sea. The rain cloud has become saturated with water vapor during the day. As the temperature falls, the vapor condenses and falls as rain.

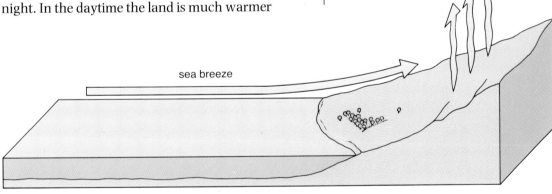

than the sea, but at night the sea is warmer than the land.

These differences in temperature between land and sea create local, daily winds called sea or land breezes. In the daytime the hot land causes air to rise above it. To replace this rising air, some cooler air is sucked from above the sea to produce the sea breeze that blows on to land. At night, the reverse happens. Warm air rises above the sea and a breeze blows off the land to replace it.

In some parts of the world, huge land masses heat up so much that seasonal, rather than daily, reversals of wind direction are caused. For example, **monsoon** climates occur in India and South East Asia, with winds blowing in

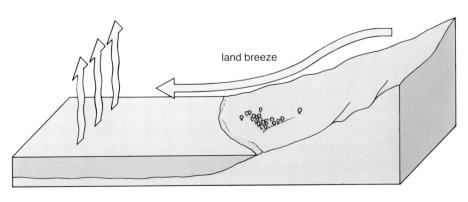

During daytime, warm air rises above the land and cooler air blows in from the sea to take its place. This is called a sea breeze. At night, the reverse happens and an off-shore, land breeze blows, as the warm air rises from the sea.

Clouds and weather systems

CLOUDS can take many forms, depending on how and where they appear. Most clouds consist of microscopic water droplets, while others are made from tiny ice crystals. There are three main types of cloud. The first is the familiar 'cotton wool' or **cumulus** cloud. Cumulus clouds heap up in clusters, sometimes forming thunder clouds, and are composed of tiny water droplets that form as moist air condenses in the cooler upper atmosphere. The second type of cloud, called **stratus**, appears as a grey, shapeless layer that extends in all directions. Stratus clouds are formed when a layer of warm, moist air flows under, or over, a mass of cold air. The third main type of cloud is seen as thin, curling wisps high up in the atmosphere. This is the **cirrus** cloud, made from ice crystals. All these clouds can combine to give other types of cloud, such as stratocumulus and cirrostratus. There are about ten varieties in all.

Clouds are often formed as a mass of land or sea is heated by the Sun and as moist air rises. This heating of land and sea also creates areas of low pressure where air is rising. Cold land or sea cools the air above and creates areas of high pressure as air sinks towards the ground.

As winds blow from high-pressure regions to low, they cause the centers of pressure to move. The low-pressure centers are called **depressions**, while the high-pressure centers are called **anticyclones**. The movement of these from day to day gives us our changing weather

Stratus clouds–from the Latin word meaning layer–form into thin layers and generally keep below a height of 2500 m.

Cirrus clouds–from the Latin word meaning curl–are seen high up in the atmosphere (above 6000 m) and are the highest of all clouds. They can be hundreds of kilometers long.

Meteorologists have to keep a constant check on air pressure, temperature and wind direction in order to predict the weather. This information is recorded at local weather stations and then passed on to weather centers. All the data gathered from weather balloons, satellite pictures and local stations is then fed into a computer to enable quick and accurate forecasts to be made.

patterns. The lines along which depressions and anticyclones meet are called **fronts.** A front is the dividing line between the cold dry air of the anticyclone and the warm, moist air of the depression. As a result of the mixing of cold and warm air, clouds form along the front and produce rain. Fronts may travel quite fast, and a period of showers can be quickly followed by bright, sunny weather. This kind of rapidly changing weather is particularly common in places like Britain, which is affected by fronts sweeping in from the Atlantic Ocean. Some parts of the world have much more steady, or stable weather. The central areas of continents in summer are usually covered by a region of low pressure as the Sun heats the land and causes air to rise. These regions may have violent thunderstorms in the evening as the hot, moist air rises into cooler air to form thunderclouds.

Meteorologists collect information on temperature, air pressure and wind direction from all around the world and plot this information on maps to help them forecast the weather. When we look at a weather map we notice the series of rings that cover the map. These are **isobars** and are drawn through points with the same atmospheric pressure. At the center of the rings, the pressure areas are marked 'high' and 'low'. These are the key to understanding weather because they represent the areas of high and low pressure. The fronts, where high- and low-pressure areas meet, are shown by lines with triangles standing for cold fronts or semicircles for warm fronts. These symbols tell us whether a front is pushing warm or cold air ahead of itself. Meteorologists use many other symbols on their maps but when you see the forecast on television the maps have been simplified to show us how much of the Sun we shall see, the strength of the wind and its direction, and what the temperature will be.

A satellite picture can be placed over the map to show quite clearly where there is cloud and the direction the cloud is moving. Such pictures demonstrate that the clouds in a high-pressure area move in spirals around the center.

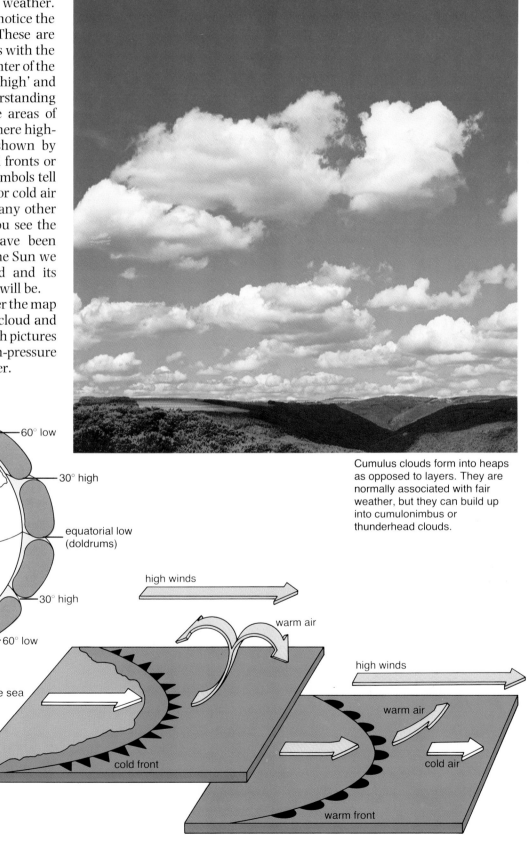

Cumulus clouds form into heaps as opposed to layers. They are normally associated with fair weather, but they can build up into cumulonimbus or thunderhead clouds.

The main pressure belts from the equator to the poles (above). When a mass of warm air passes over a mass of cold air, the line at which they meet is known as a warm front. As the warm air rises it cools and the water vapor it holds condenses into rain clouds. A cold front occurs when a mass of cold air overtakes a warm mass, forcing the warm air upwards.

polar high
60° low
30° high
equatorial low (doldrums)
30° high
60° low
polar high

high winds
warm air
cold air from the sea
cold front

high winds
warm air
cold air
warm front

Thunderstorms, tornadoes and lightning

A THUNDERSTORM starts when warm, moist air near ground level begins to rise. The air cools as it rises, and water vapor within it condenses to form cumulus clouds. As you go higher in the atmosphere, the temperature drops steadily. In winter, when the ground is cool, this rate of temperature drop is fairly small. However, in summer, heat builds up near the Earth's surface. Now the high-altitude air remains cold, and the rate of temperature drop is more rapid. It may be over 1°C for every 150 m of altitude. In winter the rising moist air cools rapidly. When it becomes colder than the surrounding air, it stops rising. In summer, the moist air remains warmer than the surrounding air, even at great heights, and the cumulus clouds soar up unhindered. Eventually, several cumulus clouds combine into a single towering cloud known as a **cumulonimbus.**

Isolated thunderclouds do occur in the summer, but on occasions a whole line of

Inside this familiar thundercloud, moist, warm air surges upwards at speeds which reach 50 kph, and may exceed 100 kph. At a height of about 14 km the rising air meets a region where the air temperature becomes warmer again with increasing height. This prevents the air from rising further, and flattens out the top of the cumulonimbus into an anvil-shaped cloud of ice-crystals.

tornadoes, where the wind speed and rotation of the supercell is greatest.

If a ball attached to a piece of string is swung around in a circle, it will speed up when pulled towards the center. Rotating winds can behave in a similar manner. A strong low-pressure center may form within a rotating supercell thunderstorm. This sucks the winds that are rotating around the outside of the storm inward, causing them to speed up dramatically. Near the center of the supercell, the winds whirl around at tremendous speeds, sometimes almost as high as 500 kph. Soon after this high-speed rotation has started, a whirling funnel extends downward from the thundercloud base. The funnel grows larger and steadily longer until it suddenly contacts the ground in an explosion of flying dirt. The tornado funnel, or **twister**, sweeps up objects on the ground like an enormous vacuum cleaner. Within a large tornado there may be two or three separate but

perhaps fifty thunderheads may be produced. This normally occurs when an advancing cold front forces itself, like a wedge, beneath a layer of warm, moist air. This causes the layer of warm air to soar upwards into colder regions. A line of cumulus clouds then forms along the line separating the two air masses. These rapidly form into a line of thunderclouds, several hundred kilometers in length, known as a **squall line**. This may sweep forward at speeds of up to 60 kph. Squall lines sometimes contain **supercell thunderclouds**, long-lived rotating storms that are particularly violent. The supercell thundercloud may give rise to

Tornado in Nebraska. Starting as a greyish-white cloud, a tornado becomes steadily darker as it sucks up more dirt. The funnel advances at between 40 and 90 kph, usually moving from southwest to northeast in the Northern Hemisphere. On average, a tornado lasts for less than 20 minutes. The power of the tornado is concentrated in a narrow band between 10 m and 300 m wide.

The upper parts of thunderclouds have a positive charge, while the lower portions contain negative charges. It is thought that within the cloud negatively charged water droplets are surrounded by positively charged ice particles. Strong air currents break these clusters apart. The lightweight ice crystals (positive) are carried upwards leaving the negative water droplets at the base of the cloud.

Lightning over Tucson, Arizona. Every year, more than 16 million thunderstorms occur on the Earth. At any moment, about 1800 are taking place at the same time. Heavy downpours of rain, or hail, usually accompany thunderstorms. A single storm can release over 500 million liters of water.

cloud has an electric potential of 12.5 million to 50 million volts, relative to the ground. At this stage a huge electrical spark between the ground and cloud is imminent.

A typical lightning stroke starts with a downward leader from the cloud. This moves in a zigzag path in steps about 50 m long, taking about 1/100th of a second to reach the ground. The stroke forms a conductive channel no wider than a pencil, connecting the ground to the cloud, and as much as 8 km long. A massive electrical current then flows up this channel from the ground to the cloud. This is called the **return stroke**. An entire lightning discharge, called a flash , may last a second or two. Each flash may contain several individual lightning strokes, causing the flickering often visible to the naked eye. The return stroke current instantly heats the narrow channel to a temperature of about 30,000°C, roughly five times the surface temperature of the Sun. The heating causes the air to expand rapidly, creating a shock wave to move outward from the channel at the speed of sound. The resulting 'sonic boom' is heard as thunder. When thunder rumbles for several seconds, you are hearing the sound produced from different parts of the stroke channel.

smaller funnels. Severe tornadoes rarely occur outside the United States, but smaller ones are sometimes seen elsewhere. These consist of hosepipe-shaped clouds, sticking out from beneath large cumulonimbus. Over water, these produce **waterspouts**, which may cause damage but are never as severe as tornado funnel clouds.

As water vapor rises up in a cumulonimbus it begins to freeze as the temperature drops to −10°C. Water normally freezes at 0°C, but high up in thunderclouds the air is so pure that water droplets can exist at temperatures well below the freezing point without turning to ice. As these super-cooled water droplets collide with tiny particles of dust and ice, they freeze to them, forming small hailstones that are buffeted up and down by strong air currents within the cloud. As this happens, the hailstones gather more layers of ice until they become so heavy that they fall to the ground, sometimes causing tremendous damage. A hailstone that fell in Kansas in September 1970 was nearly 15 cm across and weighed 0.75 kg.

Thunderstorms are normally accompanied by lightning and its noisy companion, thunder. A lightning flash is a giant electrical spark between the ground and an electrically charged thundercloud. The base of a normal thunder-

Hurricanes, typhoons and cyclones

MUCH OF OUR KNOWLEDGE of the world's weather patterns has been obtained in mid-latitudes. These are the regions in both Southern and Northern Hemispheres lying between latitudes 30° and 60°. However, half the Earth's surface lies in the band stretching across the equator between latitudes 30°N and 30°S. This region includes the tropics and the sub-tropics, and what happens here has a considerable affect on the weather in other parts of the world. As the warm air rises in the tropics and sub-tropics, cooler air moves towards the equator from the North and South Poles to replace it. Weather patterns in the mid-latitudes are a result of these air movements.

These tropical regions have weather systems which are found nowhere else on Earth. The most spectacular of these systems are the great storms or **tropical cyclones** which are very destructive. If they occur in the west Atlantic Ocean, these storms are called **hurricanes**, typhoons if they take place in the west Pacific Ocean, and cyclones in the Indian Ocean.

Other weather systems are unique to the tropics, the most common being large areas of heavy shower clouds, or thunderstorms. These occur along a belt known as the Inter-Tropical Convergence Zone, or the ITCZ for short, and the greater part of the areas of cloud and rain in the tropics is connected with the ITCZ.

Tropical cyclones are, perhaps, the most spectacular types of weather occurring on the Earth. They are also the most dangerous. Each year, they result in more loss of life than all other storms combined. Tropical cyclones begin in the steamy, late-summer heat of the tropics, which warms the oceans, and the air

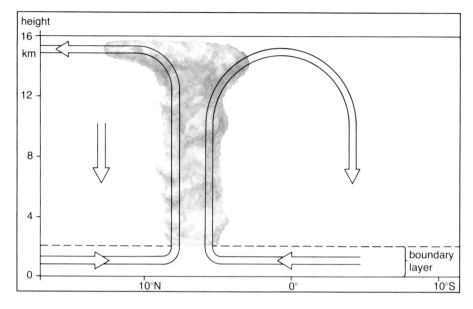

Idealized flow in the vicinity of ITCZ. Along the ITCZ, cold air masses moving inwards from the North and South Poles meet one another. At the boundary, the air from each hemisphere rises to a height of between 12km and 14km. Here the air masses once again move back towards the Poles from which they came.

Extreme seasonal displacement of the ITCZ. The ITCZ marks the boundary between the air masses of the Northern and Southern Hemispheres. This boundary is nearly always a few hundred kilometers north or south of the equator, but not along the equator itself.

immediately above. When the oceans are warm enough, high surface winds cause rapid evaporation of the sea water. The water vapor rises and eventually condenses to form clouds. Enormous quantities of heat are transferred into the atmosphere. The driving force behind the tropical cyclone is the water vapor being evaporated from the warm ocean surface. This mixture of heat and water vapor frequently forms a series of thunderstorms that may later develop into a tropical cyclone.

The trigger which sets off most hurricanes in the west Atlantic Ocean is an area of low pressure moving westward. This may have started off as a thunderstorm in West Africa. About one hundred low-pressure areas are tracked each year into the Atlantic. Less than ten of these survive to become devastating

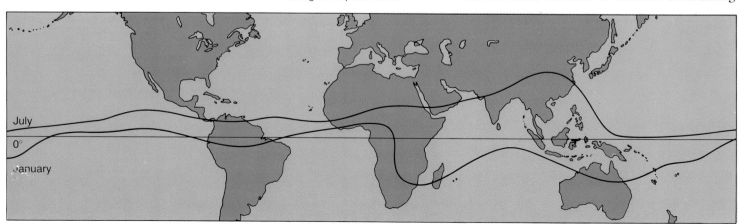

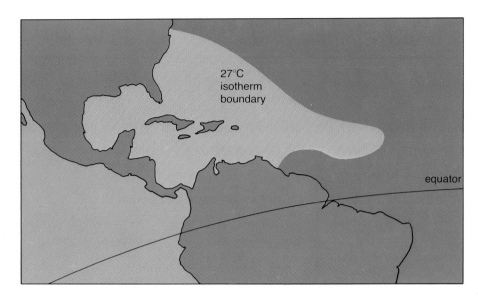

As pressure falls in the storm center, the ring of maximum wind speed decreases rapidly from about 350 km to perhaps 50 km in diameter. Outside this area the wind speed drops quickly, but within it the winds spin around at speeds of over 50 m per second (180 kph). Often the greatest damage is done, not by the wind, but by a rolling mound of sea water called a **storm surge**. This may be 8 m above normal sea level, and is pushed ahead of the storm. The surge often causes tremendous loss of life when it hits the shore. A tropical cyclone will always die out when it travels a distance inland. This is because it loses the large supply of moist, warm air, caused by evaporation from the warm ocean waters, which the cyclone needs for continued activity.

tropical storms or hurricanes. Typhoons in the western Pacific, cyclones in the Indian Ocean, and a few hurricanes in the Atlantic begin in a different way. They start off with Southern Hemisphere trade winds moving in a north-westerly direction towards the ITCZ. When they reach the ITCZ, they push a slight dent in it. In late summer, when the ITCZ is found well north of the equator, a group of thunderstorms within the dent may start spinning around. Northern Hemisphere trade winds moving in a southwesterly direction may then carry off the tropical storm which is beginning to form.

The main difference between a cluster of thunderstorms and a dangerous tropical cyclone is the speed it spins at. The spin is helped by the Earth's rotation. Any kind of spinning caused by the Earth's rotation is called the Coriolis effect, after the French scientist Gustave Coriolis, who first explained it in 1835. Near the equator, the Coriolis effect is weak. However, storms formed in the tropics can have their spins increased. If this happens, a cluster of thunderstorms may develop into a tropical storm. More warm, moist air is sucked in at low level. This rises rapidly, and the high pressure near the cloud tops pushes it outwards. A steadily deepening area of low pressure, or **tropical depression**, forms in the center of the cluster of thunderstorms. Seven out of ten of these depressions develop into hurricanes.

The depression becomes a tropical storm when its winds reach gale force, that is 62 kph.

The area shown above is one of the main breeding grounds of tropical cyclones. These can develop in areas where the surface temperature of the sea exceeds 25°C.

The central region of a hurricane *(right)*, where the pressure is lowest, is usually calm. It is known as the eye. As the center passes, the violent winds from one direction suddenly end. Then, after one or two hours of calm, there is a further period of violent winds from the opposite direction.

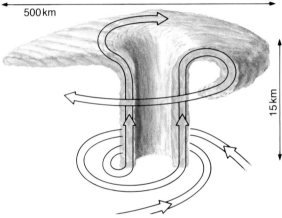

500 km

15 km

Whirling bands of rain-filled clouds converge on the eye of hurricane Gladys, as the storm gathers strength before crossing the Florida peninsula.
Photograph taken by the crew of Apollo 7 on 18th October 1968.

Weather satellites

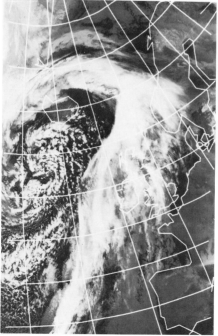

SCIENTISTS who investigate the weather are called meteorologists. To study a particular feature, such as a region of high or low pressure, and predict, or forecast, its activity, may require observations from an area as large as western Canada. On a clear day you might see cloud formations more than 40 km away from where you are standing. However, think how many hundreds of trained observers you would need to cover an area as large as that described above. By combining great numbers of observations and analyzing them by computer, it is possible to get information on large weather systems. Our knowledge of the weather has improved because the methods for making these accurate observations over such wide areas have also improved. Satellites orbiting far above the Earth's surface provide a new 'observing platform' for meteorologists. One satellite picture may show an area of over one million square kilometers.

Several different families of weather satellite are now being used. They have names such as NOAA, METEOSAT, TIROS, and METEOR, the Soviet Union's satellite series. The low-altitude weather satellites orbit at heights between about 800 km and 1100 km. Many are put into a circular **polar orbit**. They pass almost directly over the North and South Poles, at

Some weather satellites photograph the world's cloud cover as a series of slightly overlapping pictures. The satellite passes over the North and South Poles on each orbit. As the Earth rotates on its axis, the satellite is able to photograph the whole of the Earth's surface, building up a complete picture.

The two photographs below were taken by satellites NOAA 7 and 8, from a height of 850 km in December 1983. The images are in infrared with white standing for cold and black for warm. The left-hand picture shows the center of a low to the south of Iceland. The cold front of the depression is moving towards the British Isles. In the right-hand picture, taken 17 hours later, the low is dispersing and the cold front has moved further east.

about 900 km altitude. On each orbit, the television camera used on the TIROS series can cover a strip about 3500 km wide around the Earth. The strip is made up of a number of pictures taken one after the other, with some overlap between them. In this way the whole surface of the Earth may be scanned twice every twenty-four hours.

Satellites now help in all areas of weather forecasting. In local forecasting, the weather is predicted over a small area, and rarely for more than twenty-four or forty-eight hours ahead. Satellite pictures show cloud patterns over a larger area than that for which the forecast is being prepared. An experienced meteorologist can look at these pictures and check the position of the various fronts and high- and low-pressure regions on the weather map. This helps to provide more accurate regional forecasts. The television weathermen frequently show satellite pictures during their broadcasts.

Weather forecasting is also carried out on a global scale using large computers. This may require several tens of thousands of computer instructions. Calculations are made of temperature, pressure and humidity, as well as of wind speed and direction. This may be done for several levels in the atmosphere at each of over ten thousand separate points over the Earth's surface. For this type of forecast, the information provided by satellites is extremely important. By looking at weather patterns on a world-wide scale, scientists are able to produce

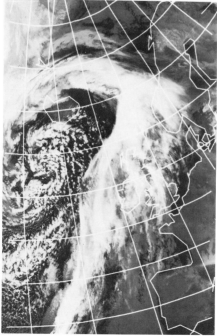

useful forecasts for a period of one to two weeks ahead.

Satellites find wind speeds at sea level by observing the movement of buoys floating on the sea. They also measure the height and distance between ocean waves. Winds higher in the atmosphere are calculated from satellite pictures which show how cloud patterns are changing. At high altitudes, satellites track special balloons which are swept along by narrow bands of fast moving air, called **jet streams**. These upper jets may have speeds of over 150 kph. Weather satellites also measure the surface temperature of the oceans, but the most accurate results are only obtained under cloudless skies. The satellite's most important tasks are the detection and tracking of powerful tropical storms. An early warning can then be provided to areas which the storms are likely to reach, and so reduce the potential loss of life.

Weather satellites collect information using the process called remote sensing. Their instruments obtain pictures of cloud patterns by two different methods. In the first, cloud pictures are taken by a sensitive television camera called a vidicon tube. This method produces pictures of the clouds in ordinary visible light, that is, light which can be detected by the human eye. In the second method, an electronic sensor is used. This detects the amount of infrared, or heat radiation, given off by the clouds, or other parts of the Earth's surface. Objects that are warm give out more infrared radiation than those that are cooler. In an infrared picture the brightest parts stand for the coolest areas, and the darkest parts of the

Tiros weather satellite, launched by a Delta launch vehicle. The solar cells, surrounding the body of the satellite, provide electricity for the instruments.

Remote sensing is used to record the temperature of land, sea and clouds. This picture of Florida, was taken at night, during the winter. The temperature variations in degrees Fahrenheit are keyed to colors, BK for black, YL for yellow, LB light blue, PK pink and DB dark blue.

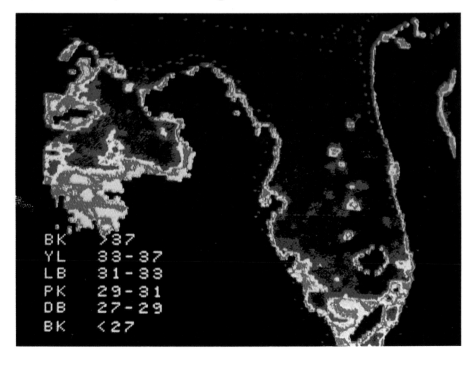

BK	>37
YL	33-37
LB	31-33
PK	29-31
DB	27-29
BK	<27

picture stand for the warmest ones. Clouds at low levels give off more infrared radiation than those which are higher and cooler. The tops of the highest clouds appear as white patches on infrared, black-and-white pictures. Lower clouds appear steadily more grey. The lowest and warmest will be darkest of all.

Infrared sensors are useful because they can operate at night as well as in daylight. In additon to measuring the height of cloud features, infrared photographs provide a great deal of other information. Air containing water vapor radiates different amounts of infrared energy from that radiated by dry air. So the detectors can be used to map areas of high and low air humidity. They can also observe high, thin cirrus clouds which cannot be observed by other methods. Areas of snow and ice cover can also be detected. This means that the advance and retreat of the polar ice-caps during the late autumn and spring seasons can be observed. In this way, the movement of icebergs, which might be dangerous to shipping, are closely watched. Infrared pictures also give information on variations in ocean temperatures. Recently it has become possible to make a film of satellite pictures taken at, for example, half-hourly intervals. By running such a film through an ordinary projector, it is easy to see the motion of cloud formations over a period of several days, taking place in less than a minute. This technique, called **time-lapse photography**, is used by meteorologists to follow the movement of large-scale weather formations around the world.

Climatic change

As we have seen, the Earth's weather is caused by continual movement of warm and cooler air masses in response to the heat energy from the Sun. This movement causes changes in temperature, pressure and amount of rainfall. These daily changes give rise to the weather at any place on the Earth. The word **climate** is used to describe the type of weather in particular regions of the Earth, over time periods which range from a few months to hundreds of millions of years.

Two types of climate are recognized today. Deep inside the great continental land masses, the difference between the highest and lowest temperatures, called the temperature range, is large and the rainfall range is quite small. This is known as a **continental climate**. An extreme example is the climate of central eastern Siberia, at the heart of the Asian land mass. At the town of Verkhoyansk, temperatures have ranged from −70°C to +36.7°C, a variation of 106.7°C. Nearer the oceans, however, towards the edges of continental land masses, places have a rather different climate. The nearby presence of the ocean reduces the range of temperatures. However, the rainfall is greatly increased. This is known as an **oceanic climate**. On the Mariana Islands in the Pacific Ocean, between 1927 and 1935 the temperature range was only 11.8°C.

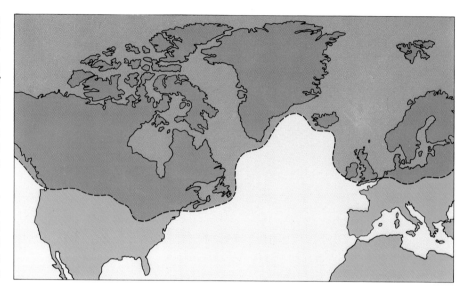

The North Atlantic in early summer, 18,000 years ago. During the last ice age, ice-sheets spread out across the North Atlantic. Most of northern Europe and North America would have looked like Antarctica today–barren, cold and hostile.

Short-term variations of the climate may cause natural disasters of vast proportions. In the tropics very low rainfall recorded several years in succession can lead to severe drought. In the tribal parts of Africa some people might lose nine out of every ten cattle and goats that they own, leading to famine.

Recently, scientists have realized that the climate at different places on Earth can change. Variations in the climate, or climatic change, have been closely studied during the last fifty years. At one time it was thought that climatic changes occurred only over geological time scales; in other words, over tens or hundreds of millions of years. Scientists think this is no longer true. Even the last hundred years have seen important changes in the climate, and scientists now believe that two different types of climatic changes are taking place. Short-term variations are changes that take place over a few decades. Long-term variations are those which have taken place over thousands or even millions of years.

Scientists have found ways of detecting changes that took place in the Earth's climate as far back as 800 million years ago. However, there is little evidence of the exact variations that took place before about 1 million years ago. We know that 40 to 60 million years ago important changes occurred in the position of the land masses on Earth. This led to great changes in the Earth's climate. Until that time there were probably no polar ice-caps, and the climate was warm everywhere. Later, the Antarctic ice grew steadily, reaching its present size about 5 million years ago. Over the past 1 million years, the Earth's climate has changed from warmer to cooler climates. These changes have taken place at periods from 100,000 to 200,000 years apart.

The Earth's climate was fairly warm between 120,000 and 75,000 years ago. This was followed by an ice age, which led to heavy ice coverage between 65,000 and 25,000 years ago. There is evidence, for example, that a great ice-sheet spread out in all directions from what is now known as Hudson Bay, and the landscape of areas such as Cape Ann, Massachussets, shows signs of having once been under such a great ice-sheet. For the past 20,000 years, the climate has generally been much warmer. The last great ice-sheets disappeared from Northern Europe about 10,000 years ago. The last stage of this ice age was marked by a period of lower rainfall in most parts of the world. Dramatic events such as ice ages take many centuries to occur. There is no question

Ancient records *(right)*, such as those of the grape harvest in France, give a clear indication of climatic change. The harvest dates show how spring and summer temperatures have varied since medieval times.

(below) The age of a tree can be determined by counting the growth rings. High up in the White Mountains of California, bristlecone pines have lived for as long as 5500 years. Scientists have examined their growth patterns and in turn have been able to establish when changes in the climate occurred.

of one taking place within the next hundred years.

The closer we approach the present day, the more evidence we find for climatic change. Between 4000 BC and 2000 BC, world temperatures were about 2 to 3°C higher than now. Some water was probably still held in small ice-sheets on the land, but there was less Arctic pack ice than now. A cooler period followed from 1500 BC to 500 BC, and then a slow warming until AD 800. Since that time, noticeable changes have taken place more frequently. A generally warm period lasted from AD 400 until about AD 1200. From 1200 until 1550 the climate was rather unstable, followed by a gradual cooling. The plagues and other diseases common in Europe between 1350 and 1600 were probably encouraged by poor summers and mild winters. There were a few harsh winters in Europe in the 1430s, but there were also warmer summers from about 1460.

The period between 1550 and 1850 has been called the Little Ice Age. During that period, glaciers moved further than at any time since the previous ice age. Also, the Arctic pack ice moved further south. At the end of the seventeenth century there was a succession of extremely cold winters and poor summers in the Northern Hemisphere. The weather was also rather dry between 1600 and 1750. During that period, plague and malaria disappeared from Europe north of the Alps. Since 1850 there has been a general warming of the climate until the present day.

The causes of climatic change

(right) Noticeable short-term variations in the Earth's weather pattern were caused by the discharge of volcanic ash high into the atmosphere, following the eruption of Mount St. Helens in Washington State.

SINCE THE END of the last major ice age, about 8000 BC, there have been between six and eight changes of climate. The effects on humans, other animals and plant life were considerable. Imagine how the lives of people today would be affected if we moved into another ice age lasting 40,000 years. Scientists are studying the causes of climatic change, and the reasons for the long- and short-term variations of climate that occur.

A major change in the Earth's climate took place 40 to 60 million years ago, when continental drift caused large movements of the land masses. Before that time, the position of these land masses prevented the waters of the oceans from flowing completely around either hemisphere. This flow of water is called **oceanic circulation**. Then, Australia broke away from Antarctica and moved northeastwards. This

When there is a burst of solar activity, sunspots can be seen. These can be as much as 100,000 km wide. Solar flares also occur and scientists believe that these have a direct effect on air movements around the Earth.

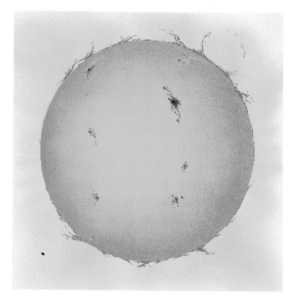

About 50 million years ago, there were probably no polar ice-caps and the climate was generally warmer everywhere. Australia and Antarctica were joined, so preventing ocean waters from flowing completely around the Southern Hemisphere. These ocean currents are very important. They can be responsible for both short and long-term climatic changes.

allowed the southern oceans to circulate completely around the hemisphere. An ice-cap began to form at the South Pole, and the Antarctic waters cooled.

The positions of the continents in the two hemispheres cause important differences in their climates. In the tropics, continents are warmer than oceans. North and south of the tropics, continents are colder than oceans. Since there is much less land in the tropics south of the equator and a lot of land near the South Pole, the Southern Hemisphere is rather cooler than the Northern Hemisphere. Although at present the Northern Hemisphere is everywhere warmer than the Southern, this might not always be true. The land masses in the Northern Hemisphere tend to form a ring around the Arctic Ocean. This separates the circulation of the polar oceans from the waters further south.

In the future these conditions may cause a colder climate in the Northern Hemisphere between latitudes 50°N and 70°N. A brilliantly white snow surface reflects the sunlight falling upon it. Large amounts of snow and ice are formed in the winter, north of latitude 50°N. If conditions were to prevent the melting of this snow and ice in the spring, then this might cause further cooling. Even larger ice-sheets would be formed. As a result, a new ice age might be started.

We tend to regard the Sun as a continuous source of heat energy, even though it is nearly 150 million km from the Earth. Certainly the Sun is very hot, with a surface temperature of 6000°C. Sometimes, on the Sun's bright surface, darker patches known as **sunspots** can be seen. Every eleven years or so, the Sun seems more energetic and there are many sunspots. Solar activity then dies down, and there are years when the Sun seems to be far less energetic. At these times, few sunspots are seen. When the Sun is most energetic, violent explosions called **solar flares** often occur on its surface. Scientists have noticed that these solar flares affect the movement of air in the Earth's atmosphere.

Variations in the Sun's output of energy are related to the numbers of sunspots and flares. If the Sun remained calm and unenergetic for long periods, important changes would occur in the Earth's weather patterns. Some scientists

Northern Hemisphere, and in the tropics, but there were also eruptions in the Southern Hemisphere from 1835 onwards.

The human race can also cause major changes in the Earth's climate. Nuclear explosions, when large quantities of dust are thrown high into the atmosphere, can have a similar effect to volcanic eruptions. Some scientists are also concerned over the use of aerosol cans for hair sprays, paints and other products. These sprays use compressed gases, called **Freons**, as a propellant. After a few weeks, the Freons may find their way into the upper levels of the Earth's atmosphere. Here they may react with a gas called **ozone** and remove it from the atmosphere. The layer of ozone in the atmosphere is vital, because it shields the Earth's surface from the dangerous **ultraviolet radiation** in the Sun's rays. Freons last for tens of thousands of years, so each push of an aerosol button may cause a bit more ozone to be destroyed. Clearly, great care needs to be taken by all of us to conserve the climate of our planet for future generations, since all life depends on it for survival.

have even suggested that the path of the Earth around the Sun might vary over long time periods, causing the distance between the two bodies to decrease or increase. The tilt of the Earth's rotation axis may also change over long periods of time. Both of these effects could lead to changes in the climate.

Volcanic eruptions are also thought to cause climatic changes on the Earth. During a violent eruption, great quantities of volcanic ash may be thrown to a height of 50 km in the atmosphere. This can have a severe effect on weather conditions. A single huge volcanic eruption might disturb the weather pattern of an entire hemisphere. The dust blocks out the Sun's rays, and this cools the Earth's upper atmosphere. If the dust is slow to clear, or eruptions continue for a long time, the effects on the climate may be severe.

We know that two periods, when the Earth's climate was much cooler than it now is, happened when there was worldwide volcanic activity. Around 500 BC there were many eruptions in both hemispheres, in places like Kamchatka, the Andes Mountains, Iceland and Tristan da Cunha. The Little Ice Age between 1550 and 1850 has also been linked with volcanic eruptions. In the 1590s and 1690s, volcanoes were active throughout the world. A veil of volcanic dust in the upper atmosphere may have cut out the Sun's energy for long periods. Most of the eruptions were in the

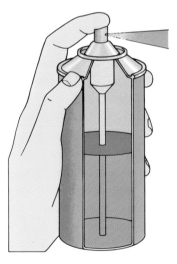

(above) Some scientists have warned that the Freon gases from aerosols could accumulate to cause harm to the ozone layer, which protects the Earth from ultraviolet radiation.

(right) Pollution from factory chimneys and motor vehicles may also affect the climate. Over a long period it is thought that the steady increase in carbon dioxide will lead to a general warming of the atmosphere.

Summary

YOU MAY THINK little is left for us to know about 'spaceship' Earth. We have followed its beginning and development as recorded in the rocks. We have seen how the rocks rose up as mountains and then became worn down by ice, water and wind. We have shown how thunder develops and clouds form. Much of this knowledge has been collected over a short period of time. Until the late fifteenth century, people thought the world was flat. Then, in 1519, Ferdinand Magellan proved them wrong by sailing around the world.

In terms of geological time it is only a 'minute' ago since scientists began to analyze our planet using scientific methods. Since the late 1800s our understanding of the world has greatly increased. Almost all the land surface of Earth has been explored and charted. In recent times we have even begun to explore the alien world at the bottom of the great oceans. We are now beginning to probe the unknown expanses of outer space.

Many of the expeditions sent to distant parts of our world are aimed at finding some new wealth. In a world hungry for energy we are constantly seeking new deposits of oil, gas and coal. With the coming of nuclear power this search is extended to include minerals from which uranium, the fuel for nuclear reactors, can be extracted. Scientists are inventing new methods and machines in order to search further into the Earth's crust. As we dig deeper into the Earth we are constantly finding out more and more about our planet. This process

The Trans-Alaska pipeline is one of the great human achievements of this century. The pipeline is 1300 km long and for the greater part of its length it is raised on stilts. This allows animals to pass underneath, which is vital for the caribou that migrate across its path. About 275,000 metric tons of oil are carried by this pipeline every day.

of exploration and discovery has been going on since civilization began. Until stone was first dug out of quarries we knew little about fossils. This discovery process continues today as we begin to reach outside our world and explore the vastness of space.

The knowledge gained from sending rockets and satellites high above the Earth has helped us in many ways. Seen from above, the weather patterns help the weathermen to make accurate predictions of future weather. Natural resources of oil and minerals can be detected by satellites passing hundreds of kilometers above the Earth's surface. These are just a few examples of ways that knowledge of our world is being increased every day.

Despite our apparent control over our world, we know that no human invention can compare with the vast power of Earth itself. If the human species were to become extinct, the Earth would still continue turning and the continents drifting. The driving force of Earth is still the same Sun which shone on the young planet 5 billion years ago. The Sun will continue to supply energy to the Earth for millions of years to come. We now have the knowledge to survive on our planet and to cope with all the problems created by ourselves over the past few hundred years. If we choose to ignore history and continue to abuse the Earth and its resources, we too, like the dinosaurs, could become extinct.

Consub, an unmanned submersible for survey work on the continental shelf, was built by the British Aircraft Corporation. The survey equipment includes closed-circuit television and cameras.

The exploration of our planet has been greatly aided by space research. Satellites scan the surface continuously, relaying information back to scientists on the ground. As well as supplying details of weather systems, satellites can help with mineral exploration, pollution, crop disasters and natural disasters such as floods and hurricanes.

Glossary

accretion: the process by which something grows in size due to a gradual build-up of *matter* deposited on it.

adapt: to change to suit new conditions.

aftershock: a smaller shock that continues to be felt for several months after the major shock of an *earthquake*.

algae: simple plants that usually live in water.

ammonite: a type of extinct shelled animal, now found in fossil form.

amphibian: an animal, such as a frog, that breeds and begins its life in water but, as an adult, develops lungs and can breathe air on land.

anticyclone: an area of *high pressure*.

asteroid: one of many thousands of small, minor *planets* travelling around the Sun. Most of them have orbits between Mars and Jupiter.

asthenosphere: a layer of the mantle beneath the stronger *lithosphere*, made up of weak material.

atmosphere: the layer of gases, *oxygen*, nitrogen and others, which surrounds the Earth.

basalt: a dark, glassy-looking rock formed by *volcanic* action.

bathysphere: a diving vessel used for deep-sea exploration.

bedrock: the solid rock beneath the soil.

block mountain: a mountain formed when the land on one side of a *fault* rises steeply above the level of the land on the other side.

body waves: the waves which travel through the surrounding rock during an *earthquake*.

Carboniferous: describes the period in the history of the Earth when a warm, damp *climate* produced great forests which gradually gave rise to the Earth's coal beds.

centripetal force: the force which attracts matter inwards, towards the center.

cephalopod: a group that includes the squids and octopuses.

china clay: also known as kaolin, a fine white clay used in making porcelain.

cirrus: a type of wispy, curly cloud that appears high in the sky.

cleavage: the way in which crystals split in definite *planes*, showing smooth surfaces.

climate: the average weather conditions in an area of the Earth.

comet: a small body in the *solar system* that sometimes has a long 'tail' made of dust and gases which reflect sunlight.

compound: a substance made up of a number of *elements*.

condense: to turn from a gas into a liquid, by cooling.

continental climate: the type of *climate* found inland, with a wide range of temperatures and a narrow range of rainfall.

continental drift: the theory that large land masses move apart because of the movements of the Earth's *crust*.

continental shelf: the shelf of land beneath the sea that slopes down gradually from the coast until it meets the continental slope.

convection currents: in geology, those currents which carry heat from the *mantle* in an upward movement.

convection cycle: the regular rising of hot *mantle* material which is followed by its falling as it cools down.

core: the center of the Earth with a liquid outer part and a solid inner core.

Coriolis effect: the way in which winds are pushed, or deflected, to the right in the Northern Hemisphere and to the left in the Southern Hemisphere.

corundum: a hard mineral; its colored varieties are ruby and sapphire.

Cretaceous: describes a period in the history of the Earth when the dinosaurs were alive and early *mammals* and flowering plants began to develop. The dinosaurs died out at the end of this period.

crevasse: a deep crack in a *glacier*.

crust: the outer layer of the Earth, made up of rock.

cumulonimbus: several *cumulus* clouds combined, from which showers of rain fall.

cumulus: a dense fluffy-looking cloud with a dome-shaped upper part.

cuticle: the strong outer covering of insects.

decay: to break down, or decompose.

delta: a triangular area at the mouth of a river formed by the *deposit* of *sediment*, as in the case of the Nile.

deposit: *(verb)* to lay down; a fast-moving river deposits any material it has been carrying along, once the current slows down.

deposit: *(noun)* a substance that is left behind by water and wind.

depression: an area of *low pressure*.

dwarf star: a star which is small, but dense, and that does not give out a great deal of light.

earthquake: a shaking of part of the Earth's *crust* as a result of the movement of rock beneath the surface.

echo sounder: an instrument for testing the depth of the sea bed; a sound wave is sent down and the time taken until its echo is picked up is then measured.

element: a simple substance that cannot be broken down further by a chemical process.

embryo: an *organism* in its first stage of life, when its cells begin to multiply after fertilization.

emery: a hard, coarse type of *corundum* used for grinding and polishing.

energy: the power to do work.

environment: the surroundings in which *organisms* live and develop.

epicenter: the place on the surface of the Earth directly above the *focus* of an *earthquake*.

erosion: the process by which fragments of rock, loosened by *weathering*, are further worn down and carried away.

evaporation: the process by which moisture is drawn off by heating and drying.

evolution: the process by which animals and plants gradually change over millions of years.

false-color pictures: these show the way in which infrared light is reflected by various objects, using different colors to show up the amount of reflection.

fault: a crack in the Earth's *crust* where one mass of rock has moved up or down.

feldspar: a mineral which is usually hard and glassy and is found in *igneous* rocks.

filament: a slender thread of wire inside an electric light bulb.

focus: the place where rocks under great pressure finally jolt apart, starting an *earthquake*.

foraminifera: single-celled sea animals whose shells are full of tiny holes and which form the largest part of chalk.

Freon: a gas used as a propellant in aerosol sprays.

front: the boundary between two masses of air of different temperature.

galaxy: a system of stars, *planets*, dust and gas forming a cluster in space. Our own galaxy is called the Milky Way.

glacier: a slow-moving mass of ice and snow that builds up on an area of constant heavy snowfall.

granite: a very hard rock made of *quartz*, *feldspar* and small quantities of other minerals.

gravity: the pulling force exerted by a mass.

high pressure: a force of air near the Earth which pushes down more strongly than usual, because it is being cooled.

hurricane: a wind, formed over the west Atlantic Ocean, which blows at speeds greater than 120 kph.

ice-cap: a mass of ice from a *glacier* that slowly spreads outwards from a central point.

ice-sheet: a thick layer of ice lying over a large area, such as was found in the ice age.

igneous: a type of rock formed by the hardening of *magma*.

impurities: traces of substances, such as metal *oxides*, which often give color to a gem or precious stone.

invertebrate: any animal that does not have a backbone.

island arc: a chain of volcanic islands that has risen up from under the sea along the edge of a *subduction zone*.

isobar: a line on a map, used to connect areas of the same atmospheric pressure.

jet streams: very rapid winds high up in the air, moving from west to east.

lapilli: pieces of rock that are thrown out of a *volcano* during a violent eruption.

laser: a device which amplifies light to produce a narrow, colored beam, with light waves all of the same *wavelength*.

lava: molten rock that erupts from a *volcano*.

light-year: the distance travelled by a ray of light in one year. It is a unit of distance, not of time.

limonite: a brownish *oxide* of iron.

lithosphere: the outer, solid rock layer of the Earth.

low pressure: a force of air near the Earth which pushes down more weakly than usual, because it has been heated by the Sun.

luster: the reflecting power of the surface of a mineral.

magma: molten rock found in the *mantle* on which the *plates* of the *lithosphere* ride.

magma reservoir: a pocket under the surface of the Earth in which molten rock collects.

magnetic field: the space around a magnet in which it exerts its force.

mammal: a warm-blooded animal, usually covered with hair, that gives birth to live young which feed on the mother's milk.

mantle: the layer immediately beneath the *crust* of the Earth, lying above the *core*.

marcasite: a mineral that looks like *pyrites* but easily powders when exposed to air.

marsupial: a type of animal, mainly found in Australia, such as a kangaroo. The female has a pouch in which the young are carried until they can feed themselves.

matter: any substance found in the universe. It cannot normally be destroyed, only changed from one form to another.

metamorphic: rocks, such as marble, formed from existing rocks by changes in the Earth's *crust*.

meteorite: a solid body from space that enters the Earth's *atmosphere* burning fiercely, the remains of which fall on to the Earth.

mica: a mineral, containing plenty of silicon, that crystallizes into layers.

mid-ocean ridges: mountain ranges between 1000 m and 4000 m below the surface of the ocean, with some high peaks which reach the surface and form islands.

monsoon: a wind which changes its direction with the seasons; the word is also used to describe the rainy season during which the wind blows from a southerly direction.

moraine: the gravel, rocks and clay left behind when a *glacier* passes.

nebula: a cloudy patch in space that consists of a *galaxy*, or of the materials, such as gas and dust, from which galaxies are formed.

Neanderthal: a type of early human who lived in caves and hunted animals, such as reindeer.

neap tides: those tides, neither very high nor very low, which happen soon after the first or third quarter of the Moon, when the Sun and Moon are at right angles, and so are working against each other.

nodules: lumps of rock found on the deep ocean floor, roughly the size and shape of a potato, surrounded by layers of metal *oxide*.

nuclear reaction: a reaction which involves a change in the nucleus, or core, of an atom. Such reactions may happen naturally or may be produced artificially.

oceanic circulation: the flow of the seas and oceans around the globe.

oceanic climate: the type of *climate* found near the oceans where the range of temperatures is not wide but rainfall is great.

oceanic crust: the Earth's surface beneath the sea, which is thinner and weaker than on land, and is regularly being destroyed with new *crust* being formed.

ore: any mineral source from which metal can be extracted.

organism: a living plant or animal.

outwash plain: an area covered in sand and gravel deposited by streams flowing from a melting *glacier*.

oxide: a chemical *compound* of *oxygen* with another *element*.

oxygen: one of the gases found in air and water. It is essential for life.

ozone: the gas found in the upper *atmosphere* which filters out the dangerous *ultraviolet radiation* from the Sun's rays.

period: in geology, the twelve divisions into which geological time is split.

placenta: also known as the afterbirth, this is a structure found in mammals, which connects the *embryo* to the mother. It allows the embryo to get its food and *oxygen* from her.

placers: riverbed deposits of gravel or sand, containing gems or heavy *ore* minerals, such as gold.

plane: a flat surface.

planet: a body in space that revolves around the Sun.

plate: a slab-like part of the Earth's *lithosphere* that rides over the lower part of the *mantle*.

polar orbit: an orbit which passes over the Earth's poles.

pyrites: a yellow mineral, also known as pyrite, which may be mistaken for gold.

quartz: a compound of silicon, it is an extremely common crystalline mineral that is hard and shiny. Some of its colored varieties are valued as semi-precious stones, and, since it is also the major part of sand, quartz is used in the making of glass.

radioactive: giving off radiant energy in the form of rays as the nucleus of an atom *decays*.

radiolaria: single-celled deep-sea animals with skeletons made of silica.

rain shadow: the 'dry' side of a mountain or high ground, where some of the drops of water in clouds, meeting warmer air, turn back into vapor and therefore do not fall as rain.

refraction: the way a ray of light is bent when it passes from one transparent material to another.

remote sensing: a process by which cameras in a *satellite* record areas of radiation on the Earth.

return stroke: the massive electrical current which flows back to a thundercloud from the ground.

ridge: in geology, a fold, or raised narrow strip where two *plates* meet.

salt: a *compound* formed when metal particles replace the hydrogen in an acid.

sandstone: a *sedimentary* rock, which is made up mainly of *quartz*.

satellite: a body that revolves around a larger one. An example of a natural satellite is the Moon, while an artificial satellite is one which has been sent up by a rocket and put into orbit.

sea-floor spreading: the process by which new oceanic *crust* is made when molten rock is forced out of the *mantle* at the edges of the *ridges* and then cools, adding to the existing ocean floor.

sea-lily: a sea animal, looking something like a flower, attached by a stalk at the end opposite its mouth.

sediment: material that settles after being carried by wind or water.

sedimentary rocks: those rocks, such as sandstone, that were formed when fragments of existing rock were removed by *weathering* and were then laid down by water, wind or ice on to the land or under water.

seismic wave: a wave of energy, formed during an *earthquake*, which passes outwards from the *focus* through the surrounding rock.

seismic profiling: a method of mapping the bed of the ocean by sending powerful sound waves down through the rocks.

seismograph: an instrument which senses the movements of the Earth's *crust* and records them. It can detect the location of *earthquakes*.

shale: a sedimentary clay rock with fine grains. It may contain oil.

sial: the light, outer *crust* of the land areas of Earth, mainly made up of *silica* and *aluminum*.

silt: a *sedimentary* material made up of particles midway in size between those of sand and clay.

sima: the part of the Earth, made up of *silicon* and *magnesium*, which lies beneath the *sial* and makes up the oceanic *crust*.

snow-field: a large expanse of snow

solar flare: a fierce, short outburst on the surface of the Sun.

solar system: the Sun and the nine *planets* moving around it in orbit. The system also includes *comets*, meteors and *asteroids*.

spectroscope: an instrument used for breaking up light and for studying the colors of the spectrum.

spring tides: those tides, both very high and very low, which happen after the new and the full Moon, when the Sun and Moon are lined up with each other, and so are pulling together.

squall line: the line of thunderclouds that forms along the *front* between two masses of air of a different temperature.

stalactite: an icicle-shaped *deposit* hanging from the roof of a limestone cave, formed by the continual dripping and *evaporation* of water full of lime.

stalagmite: a cone-shaped *deposit* growing up from the floor of a cave, often built up by drips from the *stalactite* above.

storm surge: a great wall of sea water that rides in front of a tropical storm until it reaches the land.

stratosphere: the layer above the *troposphere*, made up of thinly-spaced gas molecules.

stratus: a low-lying cloud forming a dull, grey sky.

subduction zone: a place where the *crust* of the Earth is pushed downwards into the *mantle* where it becomes molten.

sunspot: a dark patch on the surface of the Sun.

supercell thunderclouds: these produce fierce, whirling storms that may turn into *tornadoes* if they revolve fast enough in a strong wind.

supernova: a very large star in the process of destroying itself. It ends up as an expanding cloud of gas.

tectonic plates: great slabs of the Earth's *crust* which are in motion above the *mantle*, moving closer together or further apart.

terminal moraine: the gravel, rocks and clay *deposited* at the lower end of a *glacier's* path.

thermal radiation: the warmth that is felt when infrared radiation is present.

time-lapse photography: a method of taking pictures at intervals, then running them as a film so that gradual changes may be seen speeded up.

tornado: a rapidly turning, violent storm with a funnel-shaped cloud. It travels a short distance, covering a small area.

trace fossil: the shape of an animal or its home that has been preserved in rock.

transpiration: in plants, the process by which moisture passes out through the leaves and is then evaporated.

trench: a deep underwater furrow or ditch where *plates* come together.

trilobites: sea animals having the body divided into three parts, now extinct.

tropical cyclone: a system of winds blowing inwards in the form of a spiral to a center of *low pressure*, brought about by warm, moist air rising from the ocean.

tropical depression: an area of deepening *low pressure* formed along a group of thunderstorms which often becomes a *hurricane*.

troposphere: the lower region of the *atmosphere*, reaching to about 15 km above the ground.

tsunami: a giant sea wave, sometimes called a tidal wave, caused by *earthquakes* or *volcanic* eruptions under the ocean.

twister: the rapidly turning funnel of a *tornado*, or whirlwind, which extends down to the ground, and sucks up objects in its path.

ultraviolet radiation: the radiation found in the rays of the Sun, harmful to human beings.

uplift: the process by which land rises above the surrounding area.

vent: the mouth, or opening, of a *volcano* from which the molten rock, or *lava*, escapes.

vertebrate: an animal with a backbone.

vibration: a shaking movement.

volcano: a cone-shaped mountain with a large opening, or crater, at the top. From this crater molten rock, or *lava*, may flow under pressure from below.

wadi: a valley that is dry except during the rainy season, when a rush of water flows through it.

waterspout: a *tornado* which passes over water and sucks it up into a column of whirling air, full of mist and spray.

wavelength: in wave motion, the distance between the tops of two waves or the bottoms of two waves.

weathering: the process by which the action of wind, ice and water loosens particles of rock which are then carried away.

Index